This book is like get )f
awakening. Morgan ha ·f
the most vital arenas ⸌ _ ⸌e
potential. You simply can't go back to unknowing the self-
awareness you will discover along the way.
Liz Corwin, Owner and Creator of Walkabout Yoga

Morgan blasts through the excuses we make for not living fully
empowered lives. Dropping a megaton truth bomb on every
page, she pulls no punches along the way. *Powerful As F*ck* is
not a guidebook for some variant of magical thinking; it's a
roadmap for truly magical *living*!
Lee Gaitan, Award-winning, #1 Amazon author of *Lite Whines and
Laughter—Mild Rants and Musings on the Mundane*

Powerful As F*ck gives you tangible tools and patterns of
thought to summon the warrior inside of you. It will give you a
guide to make both small and big decisions that ultimately will
decide how your life will be lived. A voice that cuts through the
clutter and noise of the day, Morgan Field follows up to her first
book with a truly epic read with timeless truths that provides
readers with a path to access a reservoir of inner strength!
Alan Griffin, Surgical Neurophysiologist

Powerful As F*ck leads you down a tightrope walk to the other
side of exponential growth. Once you master the concepts
Morgan shares in this book, there is no going back. Your mind
will be opened. You will see the world through a different lens
—one that begins to show you all the ways your power exists.
Erin McCabe, Registered Nurse, Mom, Health and Wellness Coach

Deliciously blunt. Boldly unapologetic. *Powerful As F*ck* is an
uncompromising, witty, and lavishly frank invitation to get out
of your own way and into your dream life.
Theora Moench, Executive Coach and Business Consultant

Ready to bypass the excuses and get to the fun part of life? *Powerful As F*ck* gives you tools to take control of your life. It will prompt you to deal with future challenges in a more intrinsic way, thereby giving you the peace of mind.

Christopher Kenneth Thomas, Director of Recruiting and Operations, Motivational Speaker

If you are totally committed to uncovering your authentic self then this is the book that will cut through your BS and expose the real you! Buckle up!! It was uncomfortable and emotional at times but well worth it! I thought I knew myself and after reading this I found there were still some areas I was not honest with myself about. I wish everyone would read this!!

JoAnn S. Brown, Business Coach, Soar Thru Life

Powerful As F*ck logically presents the most empowered way to approach life and creates instant breakthrough for the reader. Put simply, this book is transformational. It contains a unique perspective conveyed in such a way that the expert benefits. Yet, it is written plainly enough for a novice to grasp with ease.

Nancy Rae Allen, Life and Business Coach

This book is powerful, brilliant, and vulnerable. It will help you get unstuck; face your fears and break free from the stories in your head that keep you from living an epic life full of wonder and fulfillment. Morgan steps into her power and unflinchingly speaks the truth of what held her back so that others may free themselves too.

Bill Carmody, Executive Coach, TEDx Storyteller, *Inc Magazine* Writer

No excuses, no nonsense and total magic. This book is ALL about waking up and taking your power back so you can live the life you've dreamed. I've been wanting to grow my business for a while and this book helped me realized how many excuses I had for why I wasn't reaching my goals. I was handing my power away all over the place. Now, I'm having so much fun taking responsibility for every last little bit of my life. Let's just say, game changer!

Shawna Burkhart, Relationship Coach for Trailblazing Leaders, Founder of The Honest Edge

If you are determined to live a life you love by claiming the power that is yours, create a permanent place on your bookshelf for this book. *Powerful As F*ck* pulls back the curtain to reveal your long-forgotten, self-limiting patterns and beliefs and hands you your power back. It will redefine everything you thought you knew about responsibility. Do you choose to shine a spotlight on your true magic and step into all that you are? If the answer is yes, you're in for an epic ride, my friend!

Ilena Adamson, Life Coach and Literary Enthusiast

Morgan's clear explanations, relatable analogies, and crucial questions will have you working on yourself even as you sleep. Situations of the past will take on a new meaning. All the power you will ever need is right here, in your hands, as you hold your copy of *Powerful As F*ck*.

Elaine Grace, Master NLP Life Coach at Recalibrate to Great. Unapologetic Epic Sexy Tribe Sister. Fabulous New Mummy!

Powerful As F*ck is direct and brutally honest, providing practical steps to make the changes necessary to uncover your own power. This book will wake you up to poisonous behaviors that hold you back and will introduce ways of thinking that make your mind your greatest friend and asset.

Melissa Coglianese, Entrepreneur, Global Business Leader at LinkedIn

Powerful As F*ck is a step-by-step guide to your awakening process and will assist you with standing in your power. You will understand how taking responsibility for your life will shift you into powerful awareness and lead you into a new life.

Tiffany Nicole, Founder of I Am Tiffany Nicole, Life Coach and Author

This book is powerful, poignant, and on-point. *Powerful As F*ck* shines a light on patterns, thoughts, and actions that seem to be "no big deal"—the same things that turn out to be the core of what's holding you back. This book leads you to examine the part you are playing in your life situations and to recognize the absolute necessity of taking responsibility for all of it.

Julie Scott, Pro Age Life Coach, Author, and Founder of "It's About Time Baby!" Coaching

Powerful As F*ck is for anyone who is ready to experience the freedom that comes with stepping into their power and owning it like a boss. It's also for anyone who knows it is time for change. Once you pick up this book, you'll wonder why you waited so long to step up as your epic, powerful self. You will be empowered to look your excuses square in the eyes, realizing you are the only one standing in your way.

Lana Williams, Life and Relationship Transformation Coach, Founder of Look With Me Coaching

Whether you're new to discovering your soul path or already diligently excavating the wisdom of your life, *Powerful As F*ck* is a must-read. It provides opportunity after opportunity to identity where you have handed away your power or taken on responsibility that belongs to others. By consistently applying the concepts in this book, readers gift themselves the magic of intentionally creating extraordinary and fulfilling lives, on *their* terms.

A.R. Strong, Reiki Practitioner, Life Coach, Author of *Sacred Awakening: Healing on My Journey of Cancer*

This book will help you to identify subconscious patterns of self-sabotage. Morgan has a remarkable ability to tell it like it is while giving you insightful tools that you can implement immediately. You can't help but examine your own limiting beliefs and habitual behaviors from a brand new perspective.

Jennifer Knappe, Owner, Cedar Creek Custom Homes

Life is too precious to sit around and repeat the same patterns. *Powerful As F*ck* sheds light on the realities of what is keeping you stuck. It helps you peel back the layers and find your truth.
Diana Hernandez, Founder and CEO of Grieve and Live, Coaching

Inside this book are the secrets to owning your life. The witty, inspiring *Powerful As F*ck* will help you empower yourself and make the desired changes you fear. I recommend reading and re-reading this book at every up-level of your journey.
Dr. Cristian Pavel, Dentist, Yoga Instructor, Co-Founder of Revive the Dream Wellness Retreats

Morgan Field is a genius generator of soul transformation. This book shines a brilliant light on the most destructive and creative force in the universe—you. *Powerful As F*ck* is a step by step Awesomeness Awareness toolkit to manifest a world beyond your wildest imaginings. Accept the invitation. Be Power Full.
Michelle Royal, Founder of RIDG, Professional Bodybuilder, Author

This book is a wake-up call! It's a game-changer for those seeking to transform their lives from the inside out. *Powerful As F*ck* is a must-read for anyone who is not yet living the life they were meant to live! It is for those who are willing to take a hard look at their self-talk and subconscious beliefs.
Kalena James, LCR Coaching LLC, Leadership Psychologist and Life Strategist Coach

This book will entertain and enlighten. It will transform how you think about power and help you reclaim it. Especially invaluable for those who have codependent tendencies, it will have you laughing out loud at yourself and digging deeper with the empowering questions Morgan provides.
Jane Kim England, CPC, ELI-MP, Empowerment Life Coach, Founder of WE Matter Worldwide, Author of *Not So Plain Jane: A Memoir*

Powerful As F*ck requires that you own your shit so you can have the time of your life. You will radically redefine what power is and learn how you can reclaim yours now.

Cora Boyd, Dating Coach, Cora Boyd Coaching

Powerful As F*ck is a masterstroke of discovery and relatability. You will walk away with a next-level resolve that you can own any situation and lead with success.

John Drumgoole Jr., Award-winning Author, *Forbes* Contributor

Morgan unapologetically calls us out for routinely giving away our power and gives us the confidence to take it back.

Nick J Murphy, Best-selling Author, *Unboxed*

Morgan's done it again! If you find yourself asking, "What can I do better? WTF can I do to get myself out of this rut, and WHY am I in this rut?" *Powerful As F*ck* gives you an in-depth look at *you* and what to do to be true to yourself!

Jason Klugh, Founder/Inventor, Freehand Drink Caddy

Ready to honestly look to yourself as the cause and solution for the current circumstance of your reality? *Powerful As F*ck* puts the opportunity to make better choices in your hands. It will change your life if you are brave enough to apply it.

Sivan Katz, Intuitive Love Coach, CPC ELI-MP

This book is a manual for anyone contemplating a new start or attempting to find the right path forward. It is for those who need a bright-light reminder that we can't control this life's unpredictable circumstances, but we can choose our thoughts and reactions to them. After reading this book, you will be able to reassess the underlying issues in your world. If you read closely, you may be able to find solutions to the said issues.

KAT V, GirlBoss at VIPviolin.com

POWERFUL AS F*CK

*Own Your Sh*t.*
Live the Life of Your Dreams.

You are more powerful
than even your wildest
Dreams!! :)

XoXo, Morgan

MORGAN FIELD

P.S. Bookmark & Magnet Included

POWERFUL AS F*CK
Own Your Sh*t. Live The Life Of Your Dreams.

Epic Sexy You Publishing

ISBN 978-0-9972224-0-1 Print
ISBN 978-0-9972224-4-9 E-Book

DISCLAIMER. This book is a work of nonfiction of the self-help, personal growth variety. The author has not used names, invented characters, or fabricated events. This book is about finding and owning your power. The author has used stories from her past to demonstrate ways she was falling short in owning her power. She has described relationships to the best of her knowledge and recollection. She has included her own perceptions and interpretations of what each relationship represented to her. These descriptions are naturally subjective in nature. Other parties have their own interpretations of what the relationships meant to them and how she appeared to them.

She has included examples that describe how she lost perspective, and therefore power, while in these relationships and also provides examples of how she learned to recognize and overcome her self-imposed "powerlessness" in order to own her power and become the person she is today. The author is not a licensed healthcare or mental health provider, nor is she a licensed therapist. Any labels or descriptions used are merely illustrative of how the author personally viewed those relationships with the lens and perspective she had access to at that point of her life.

The author has made every effort to ensure the information herein was correct at press time, the author does not assume and hereby disclaims any liability to any party for any loss, damage, or disruption caused by errors or omissions, whether such errors or omissions result from negligence, accident, or any other cause.

Printed in the United States of America

AUTHOR WEBSITE
www.EpicSexyYou.com

POWER
CONTENTS

THE ALCHEMY OF FEAR: TRANSMUTE FEAR INTO POWER 185

BECOME A BADASS AT FAILURE & PERSISTENCE 203

BE A BOSS OF TIME 211

THE VORTEX OF TRUTH 229

III. RECAP 237

LET'S RECAP, SHALL WE?! 239

HOW TO SQUEEZE THE JUICINESS OUT OF THIS SOUL BOOK 243

Born Knowing

We walk into this world as divine, majestic, and innately powerful beings. We are born fully owning our uniqueness, with our soul gifts built in, ready to grace this world as the unapologetic Who that we authentically are. We are present and joyful, limitless and fully connected to our desire. We do not question whether we are worthy of love, abundance, and the fullest expression of life. We do not doubt our power or authority.

We are born knowing.

And yes, that is me in that picture. Born knowing that I am powerful as f*ck.

INTRO

The Power Entanglement Journey

At some point on our journey through life, most of us begin to form a relationship to power that is of this human existence. Over time, we begin to lose sight of our true knowingness of our worth and power. We begin to look to the outside world to shape who we are. Almost without realizing it, we become servants to expectations and shoulds. We give in to shame and fear. We give way to familial, cultural, and societal norms. We shrink.

We begin to experience life happening to us, subconsciously creating perspectives of victimization and powerlessness. We lose trust in our own ability to know how to be who we truly are. Slowly but surely, we become disconnected from an internal sense of power and begin to look to the world around us for information about our identity. We contort ourselves to fit into the molds available to us and the image reflected back by the world around us. We conform.

As we become more and more conditioned by the external world, we develop a subconscious relationship with power. Some of us learn that power is something we need to earn, so we hustle to prove our worth. We get busy chasing paths to power that the world subliminally shows us is the road to earning our worth. We do what is expected of us. We fall in line.

Others quickly learn that power is something that must be suppressed and hidden at all costs. *Be a good girl. Be a good boy. Don't be too much.* We catch the true meaning when compliments are laced with a subtle message to dim our lights. *You are gifted. You have it easier than most people.* Sometimes the messages are overt. *Tone it down. Keep it quiet. Don't brag. Don't make people feel bad.*

You do your best, Goldilocks style, to fit in. You shrink your powerful, expansive, gifted self into whatever "just right" size box will allow the world to tolerate you and not be triggered by your greatness. You spend your life tiptoeing around others and trying your best not to make anyone else feel less than by your being *too much.* Or you avoid your power altogether.

You may even have gotten mixed signals, absorbing both of those messages. If so, your subconscious relationship with power likely became a tug of war and a dizzying push-pull that had you hustling for your worthiness and avoiding your "too muchness" at the same time.

No matter which dance you are doing with power, I can assure you that at some point it will get old. You will start to crave more for your life. In moments of clarity and full consciousness, you are able to reclaim a thread of remembrance. You catch a quick glimpse of the glimmer of knowingness you had in the beginning. You begin to see that there is another way to navigate owning your power that does not require you to earn your worth or hide who you are.

Then, one fine day, you step into the Vortex of Truth and you take your power back. Let today be that day. Welcome to a whole new world where infinite possibilities await.

P.S. Drop your email on the Epic Sexy You website to make sure you are in the know for details on how to tune in to the *Powerful As F*ck* Podcast that is currently in the soul cooker. Visit the website at www.epicsexyyou.com for deets.

POWER QUOTE

*Our deepest fear is not that we are inadequate.
Our deepest fear is that we are powerful beyond
measure. It is our light, not our darkness that
most frightens us. We ask ourselves, Who am I
to be brilliant, gorgeous, talented, fabulous?
Actually, who are you not to be?...*

*Your playing small does not serve the world.
There is nothing enlightened about shrinking
so that other people won't feel insecure around
you. We are all meant to shine, as children do.*

*We were born to make manifest the glory...
that is within us. It's not just in some of us;
it's in everyone. And as we let our own light shine,
we unconsciously give other people permission
to do the same. As we are liberated from our own
fear, our presence automatically liberates others.*

Marianne Williamson

POWER

Heeeyy, look at me. I am so powerful!

Moments of Awakening

For most of my life, I was blindly following a path to power that wasn't even mine. It was unnecessarily costing me a lot— mentally, physically, emotionally, and spiritually—and I had *no* clue. You may not have the same story as me, but I can assure you that you have adopted patterns and followed paths to power that do not serve you and that rarely lead to true power.

It is time to take your power back.

The path I blindly followed included climbing the corporate mountain. For six years, I set my sights on getting to the top. Then one day I arrived. I stood at the peak, satisfied and in complete and total awe of my accomplishments. I had the title I had always dreamed of. I had a ton of money in my bank account. I had a car that was paid off, no debt, and a gorgeous condo. I was living the dream.

I felt amazing!! For about two days. After the second day there at the pinnacle of success, the fulfillment started to fizzle. I had spent years imagining how life would be once I reached the top. Yet, here I was experiencing a cold, sobering truth of a moment where I realized I had sacrificed six years of my life for two days of fleeting fulfillment. I started thinking, "Oh my God, this cannot possibly be what power means?!"

I was so confused.

I had done everything I thought I was supposed to do in order to finally claim the power society promised if I dutifully followed the path that had been laid out for me. I graduated from high school, went to college, got a degree, and got a great job. I put in my time. I made my career #1, and I gave well over 40 hours every week. In an effort to show how committed I was, I rarely used vacation time. I chased the promotions, played the office politics, and climbed the corporate ladder. I sacrificed whatever was necessary so that I could enter the promised land of fulfillment.

Here I was, making more money than I even knew what to do with. I was at the top of my company. I had job security, a healthy 401K, and epic health benefits. I had three full weeks of vacation every year and an all-expenses-paid company trip once a year. According to the path I was guided to and the definition of power I had bought into—prestige, money, title, job security—I was winning at life, right? Wrong.

I was exhausted. Depleted. I was single and cycling in and out of toxic relationships with emotionally and/or geographically unavailable guys. At one point I was 35 pounds overweight and had five separate autoimmune-associated disorders. And, as you can see in the picture, I was literally passed out a lot of time.

The picture truly is such an on-point representation of how I was living—or not living—at that time in my life. I had to take Benadryl regularly for constant allergy attacks and chronic sinus inflammation. Then, I would relax after a week of 18-hour work days and blow off steam by treating myself to a bottle of wine. The whole bottle. All to myself, of course.

Passing out was the natural result. It was a repeatable and ongoing result. I was sleepwalking through life. *Hey, look at me. I am so powerful!* No. Clearly, this is not power.

In that first moment of waking up to this realization, I decided that I had had enough of "their" way—society's way, my family's way, the way presented by anyone and everyone who had ever directed me on to this path, *the* path, to power. I decided it was time to go off-roading and far from what had led me here. I was going to pave my own path—one that would feel good to me and one that did not require me to sacrifice my body and time or my life and the living of it in order to have mere moments of temporary fulfillment. I knew there was more to life, and I was ready to find it. Or, rather, for the first time in my existence, I was ready to create a life of true power and purpose.

Then one day, as I began to awaken further and explore new possibilities of what power could actually mean, I had a spiritual practitioner ask me a simple question that completely changed the trajectory of my life. As an outsider looking in, she could see so clearly something that I could not yet see. Instead of simply telling me what was happening, she wisely asked me a question that helped me awaken to new states of consciousness on my own.

"Morgan, do you think you're lovable?"

I can still feel the waves of profound confusion that overcame me when she posed that question. I remember thinking, *I'm independent. I'm a high-achiever. I'm a go-getter. I'm good at what I do, and I make a lot of money doing it. But am I lovable? What does that even mean?* I began to consider things further. I mean, how the hell is it that we are asked questions such as, "How is school going? How is work going? Are you getting good grades? Are you in line for that next promotion?" Yet, most of us go our entire lives never even being asked how we genuinely feel about ourselves. No one stops to ask, "How are you experiencing yourself in this journey of life?"

Am I lovable?

As much as I tried, I could not get the word "yes" to come out of my mouth. The truth was, if I had said yes in that moment, it would have been a big, fat, colossal lie. The truth was, I didn't feel lovable. Yet I had never been asked a question like that before, so I had *no clue* that I did not feel lovable until that very moment when I was confronted with this powerful question.

My mind was spinning. How the hell was it that I had figured out how to make a ton of money, get every promotion I had ever sought out, create a debt-free life, and build a rock-solid reputation that landed me epic job security, but I had never once stopped to consider how I felt about myself along the way? How is that even possible?! Here I was, smack dab in the middle of epic "success" and confronted with a question that would be one of the most profound moments in shifting my path and moving me in the direction of understanding true power. It was like touching a wound I never knew was there and then recoiling from it, only to discover an absolute goldmine of insight.

More and more, I started to realize that I had spent most of my life trying to fill inner voids or numb feelings of emptiness, unworthiness, and unlovableness with things from the outside world. Money. Titles. Achievements. Whatever it took. I would seek out love, respect, acceptance, and praise. I was constantly seeking the approval and validation of *others*, all the while thinking that when I had it, it would yield the internal power, peace, love, and delight that I craved to experience in my life.

Yet, there I was: exhausted, depleted, and sick as hell. I was overweight and alone. I could not answer "yes" to a question that seemed so simple.

Do You Think You Are Lovable?

Along the journey to owning my power, I discovered that until you learn that power comes from within, nothing works. Nothing.

Until you learn that the deepest intention of this whole life adventure is to love being you, you don't really know power at all. Life is truly about how much time you get to spend loving being you and how much you truly love the life you are creating. Until you know that, you will be chasing illusionary paths to power and fulfillment. Until you love yourself and your life, you'll subconsciously use outdated models and definitions of power that come at way too high a cost. You will inevitably sacrifice years of your life for fleeting moments of fulfillment.

So, for me, owning my power meant taking the leap. I left the $250K a year behind to follow my heart's pull to become a life coach. I left the great benefits, the healthy 401K, the perceived job security, and all of the other illusionary comforts that came with playing it safe and living a life that someone else had mapped out for me.

I am not sharing numbers and specifics to brag, but rather for you to see that I had a lot of reasons to stay in the old path to power. More than 250 thousand of them. Yet, once I had a taste of the feeling of freedom that came from awakening to the true possibilities of power, it became more and more impossible to continue sleepwalking through my life. This is my deepest hope for you: that no matter how many logical reasons you have to stay in your old path, you find the courage within to honor your own pull toward the knowingness that life has so much more to offer you than what you've had access to up until this point.

People thought I was crazy when I took the leap. Man, I even questioned my own sanity at times. But, for the first time in my life, I started to let the inner whispers take up more space than the chattering of others and the clamoring voices of doubt, fear, and conformity inside my head. I stopped listening so intently to the outside world. I stopped chasing things outside of me.

Instead, I started to listen to my soul. I began to follow a path to power guided by me, one that allowed me to define what power meant on my own terms. When I finally gave myself permission for it to get to feel good to be me—mind, body, and soul—I got to be a version of me that I loved being. Now, I get to do work that truly feeds my soul, and I have created a day-to-day life that is beyond my wildest dreams.

There is a whole new stratosphere of possibility for what power can look and feel like. It's some next level, juicy, magical goodness, and I'm going to share it all with you! After identifying the true sources of power and awakening to new possibilities of what power actually means, I am now genuinely and truly *living*.

I healed all five autoimmune-associated disorders. Gone. My body was literally showing me I was off my own majestic path, and I had no idea until I gave myself permission to pave my own way. I shit you not, the moment I started listening to myself was the very moment my body began to heal.

I realized that in my old construct of power, where power was about money, title, status, acquiring things and consisted of competing, comparing, and seeking validation from the outside world, I was lost. Who I was got lost in my hustle to be liked and the desperate desire to be taken seriously. In my quest to fit in, I lost myself in people pleasing, endlessly contorting myself to fit who others thought I should be. I was overfunctioning in every relationship and overgiving at the expense of my own well-being.

What's more, I was accidentally stealing other people's power by owning what wasn't even mine in the first place. I was handing my power away like a hot potato because I didn't even know what was mine to own. The kicker was, I was not even consciously aware I was doing any of it.

Now that I understand what true power actually is and have untangled myself from the conditioning of the outside world, I am no longer consumed with fitting into that world. In fact, I now give myself permission to stand out. I am no longer lost. I know who I am. I embrace who I am. I consciously create my life.

I no longer do shoulds and obligations. I gave those up. I swapped shoulds for desires. Instead of worrying about what the world outside of me thinks, I go inside. I ask myself: *What do I want? Who do I want to be? What would allow me to love being me even more?* These questions have led me to truly living.

If I can do it, so can you.

TAKE YOUR POWER BACK!

Swap your shoulds for desires.
Ask yourself what it is you really want.

#powerfulAF

No matter where you are in life or what you choose to do, there is a way to do it that does not entail you losing yourself. In my journey of hustling for my power and seeking to gain my worthiness from the outside world, I learned that I can have all the money and prestige in the world, be at the very top of a company, have no debt and few concerns—yet, if I do not love being me, what is the point of it all?

If you do not love who you are, what you do, how you spend your days, and who you spend your days with and if you are not proud of how you show up every single day, then you will be eternally lost. You will find yourself constantly seeking a path to power that leads you on a never-ending search for fulfillment. With this approach to life, true fulfillment will show up about as often as and be as fleeting as a solar eclipse. It may show up every few years and last for mere moments.

While your story may not be the same as mine, you most certainly have your own version of conditioning from the outside world. Deep down, you know this does not serve you.

TAKE YOUR POWER BACK!

Where are you getting in your own way? Where are you blocking your full experience of the prismatic possibilities of what owning your power can actually be like?

#powerfulAF

Together we are going to unpack that conditioning. You are going to know what is truly yours and what is not. The journey ahead will reprogram your neural pathways. You will untangle what power actually means to you. You will become the Master Creator of your life. Beginning right now, I invite you to take your power back and create your life consciously and purposefully, living wide awake and with the absolute intention of loving who you are. That is true power.

You get to decide what path you take. When you do, find the courage within to create that path consciously. You get to decide who you show up as in every single moment of every single day. When you do, find the courage within to take full responsibility for that power. Use it wisely.

Finally, remember that the outside world may give you 250 thousand or more logical reasons to keep sleepwalking through your life. In your own moments of awakening, when you are tempted to turn a blind eye to new possibilities and go back to the old ways in the name of being logical and practical, I ask you to consider this question:

TAKE YOUR POWER BACK!

How much more time are you going to allow to pass you by before you finally give yourself permission to take a new path that can lead you to mind-blowing magic? Choose power. Choose you.

#powerfulAF

Some people will keep turning a blind eye and never awaken. Some of us will choose to be powerful. Power is a choice.

If you are ready to step into a place where you get to be enough no matter what happens, where you are no longer thrown off by the world around you, where you can make decisions from want tos versus have tos, where you get to trust yourself to navigate your own path, and where you can stop hiding your gifts and your powers and can instead be unapologetically you, then read this book cover to cover. Then, read it again.

Take your power back. Live the life of your dreams.

It is time to reclaim your birthright of unshakable knowingness of self and worth, to truly and fully live your most epic, legendary life. Together we will take an intentional journey of awakening to a new kind of power. Please allow this majestic, soul creation of a book to be a conduit that provides loving truth bombs into awakening to the most amazing, juiciest life beyond your wildest imagination.

TAKE YOUR POWER BACK!

Power is juicy. It really is.
But only when it is an inside job.
Tap the power within.

#powerfulAF

It's time to take the leap into a whole new world that is waiting for you—a world where you are the Master Creator of your life, navigating it all from the inside out. Let's take that journey together and go to where your true power awaits, shall we?

Triggers Are a Gateway to New Possibilities

Before we begin, I need to warn you. The truth will piss you off. Whenever you are feeling triggered by anything in this book, remember this: triggers are a gateway to new possibilities and the birthplace of new points of consciousness. The only way to get the growth being offered to you is to step through the threshold and onto the other side where treasures await you.

Let the triggers serve as the very sign that you are onto the most epic growth you've ever experienced. Celebrate every trigger.

This book is for those courageous enough to take the training wheels off. To be willing to fall and get back up over and over and over again so that you can actually feel and experience the depths of life and all that it has to offer you. It is time to truly experience living as opposed to playing it safe.

TAKE YOUR POWER BACK!

It is time. You are ready. You've so got this, and you are so worth it.

#powerfulAF

I live what I write, although never in a state of perfection. I do battle with, snuggle up to, and dance with my own inner demons. I am continuously stretching into and striving toward more and more expansion, so that I can keep pioneering new paths of possibility for myself and for the world. I wrote this book in genuine love and with a deep desire for you. I want you to be able to expand into the "more" that your soul is calling you into.

It is magical and juicy in this lane of power that you will be walking into as we journey together. Along the way, you will need to face your own darkness and do the work. It is no accident that our worlds collided. You were guided here—right here, right now —for a profound shift of consciousness. You will shed old layers of you and mourn them. You may resist your growth. It's OK. This is normal. It is part of your metamorphosis. *Keep going!*

When I do my job as an author right, helping you shift wildly into new terrains of possibility, your Ninja Mind will turn on me.

Your Ninja Mind is the version of you that feels that its sole job is to keep you safe. "Safe," aka stuck, in the land of complete and absolute certainty. That perceived safety and an addiction to certainty keeps you locked in the status quo. It brings to a sudden stop any attempt to move toward the deep, lasting change that stepping into your power and greatness requires.

The Ninja Mind is like a tiny little Ninja that runs around your mental thought space assassinating anything that may walk you into your power and your greatness—you know, things like your dreams, your desires, change, expansion, or evolution. The Ninja Mind will resist the gifts of consciousness and the majestic responsibilities of your true power because of the discomfort it experiences in their presence. It knows that you will have to grow and change, facing constant unknowns, in order to be able to get to a whole new stratosphere.

As a result, your Ninja Mind will try to lie to you. It will tell you all sorts of things about me (the messenger) that are not true. The lies will be a means of you getting to bail on your own soul work and not take responsibility for your own choice to sacrifice your dreams.

It would be so much easier for the Ninja Mind to blame me for you not stepping into your power than it would be for you to admit to yourself that you are choosing fear over your dreams. Your Ninja Mind may lie and say that I am judging or shaming you, that somehow I don't know what I am talking about. It will convince you that I am so different from you that what I am saying is not relevant to you. It will tell you to just put the book down and walk away. *Beware the Ninja Mind!*

In its addiction to certainty it assassinates any and all attempts to move forward, as it wants you to stay nice and comfy, avoiding any and all struggle or discomfort that you will inevitably face if you stretch and grow. It's trying to skip the struggle, which is the gateway to juicy living!

Here is what I have to say to your Ninja Mind: I myself have personally gone through every single guided exercise in this book. The truth bombs that exploded into my consciousness as a result of the work I have done were palpable. I tell you this because there will be a temptation to believe that I am preaching from a high tower. You will believe that I am somehow judging you or shaming you for where you are in your life. You will think I am telling you that you are doing it "wrong."

I can assure you of this: not only am I not judging you, but I am writing this book with so much love and with the greatest desire for you to choose to go through your own darkness so that you can step into your power and join me on the other side. There, you will experience the most epic light imaginable. As my bestie said when reading this book and experiencing her own truth grenades, "The only way out is through." So when you are tempted to set this book aside, challenge yourself to keep going. Because here's the thing: *you are so worth it!*

TAKE YOUR POWER BACK!

In moments when your Ninja Mind is feeling judged or shamed, ask yourself, "How might I be judging or shaming myself?"

#powerfulAF

Power Play

Get out your journal. Let's take a deeper look at what the experience of shame has to teach you now.

+ How are you **projecting this belief** that you are being judged or shamed outward onto others as a means of protecting yourself from change and avoiding entering into the discomfort of growth?

+ Where else in your life is that **pattern** showing up?

+ Where else are you choosing to **project your fears** rather than face them?

The moment you take ownership for your fears and shame, you will take your power back. And, please, don't hand me the power of your projections. I would much prefer that you keep your power and stand in your power alongside me. That is the intention for this book. I am not judging you. I am *with you* in this human experience thing.

What I know to be deeply true is that you are absolutely superhuman! You are capable of things that the current version of you cannot even comprehend. When you choose courage over comfort enough times in life, you become unstoppable. Just remember all of this when your Ninja Mind turns on me. You think it won't happen, but I can assure you that it will.

POWER QUOTE

So often we pretend we have made a decision, when what we have really done is sign up to try until it gets too uncomfortable.

Jen Sincero

Yes! This kind of power requires your full commitment up front. You must find the courage to walk through the darkness until you find the light on the other side. In those moments of epic discomfort, when you are thinking about giving up on yourself and your Ninja Mind starts to chatter, remember that no one is powerful enough to derail you unless you let them. Not even you.

POWER QUOTE

Comfort and growth cannot coexist.

Ginni Rometty

Decide ahead of time to be all in. Take naps. Take breathers. Take breaks. Fall down and get back up over and over and over again. Question your sanity. Laugh. Cry. Throw temper tantrums.

Just don't quit on you.

TAKE YOUR POWER BACK!

True power is a choice. Will you dare to dive into the unshakable depths of awakening or will you live a life on the surface? Are you ready to choose your dreams over your fears?

#powerfulAF

Power Untangled

Let's talk about untangling and dismantling the conditioning of Power in today's world, so that you can begin to consciously create your own path in life. Why is this so important? Because it opens up so many doors to new possibilities. It introduces you to profound and empowering ways to connect with and relate to yourself and others. When you untangle yourself from others, you get to be free. That freedom is the birthplace of new depths of love, connection, intimacy, wealth, and abundance beyond your wildest imagination.

We will explore what is yours so that you can own it more fully and become the true creator of your life. We will explore common power traps and play with tools that will help you unlearn the conditioned programming of disempowerment. We will also explore what is *not* yours so you can set yourself free from all that is weighing you down.

When you master these skills, you will finally allow others their own gold mines of growth, which you have unknowingly been taking from them. Once you know these things, you cannot unknow them. Fair warning: you are now leaving the Land of Ignorance Is Bliss. You are walking into the true foundation of an unshakable power that the world around you forgot to tell you about.

Until now. That's why we're here.

Literally every single question that is sprinkled in throughout this magical divine journey together is intended for you to sit with, journal about, feel out, and answer honestly. Allow every question mark to be signal for you to pause. Explore the questions. Highlight them and build in time to answer them before rushing on to the next section. Every question is intended as an opportunity to create new neural pathways that support your growth and expansion. They will lead you to profound and even legendary personal power.

Remember, this is not a one and done kind of book. This is a book built for intentional repetition and mastery. You can read a page or a small section at a time and simmer on it. Then, you can read it again the following day and you will feel, hear, see, and experience new insights. This is a book you come back to over and over and over and over again. And, trust me, you will want your friends and family to read it too, because once you know this magical shit you will want to surround yourself with others who know it too. Treat your loved ones to a copy of the book and gift them the same consciousness and awareness you are cultivating.

As a society we tend to be conditioned to read for learning and discovery, yet reading something once is just scratching the surface. In true mastery, the art of repetition offers the greatest reward. Commit to mastery. Literally highlight anything and everything that stirs a "wow" or a "what?" or a "mmm." Capture it. Write it down and explore it more deeply.

I promise you that after you navigate the truth bombs in this book, you will love your life even more. You will feel freer, lighter, and more powerful. I will walk you into a treasure chest of tools of discovery and exploration that will allow you to genuinely understand how to take your power back. I promise not to leave you hanging. You will be provided with the essential elements of what you need to get the power party started, but first we must rip the bandaid off and enter into the Vortex of Truth.

POWER QUOTE

*Before the truth can set you free,
you need to recognize which lie
is holding you hostage.*
Unknown

I

RESPONSIBILITY
IS POWER

RESPONSIBILITY IS POWER AND THE KEY TO FREEDOM

POWER QUOTE

You are the cause of your own joy or your own misery. You hold that power. You are your own friend and your own enemy.
Swami Satchidananda

Let's talk about something that seems to be missing in today's mainstream society. This something is an absolute and total game changer. It is the fact that responsibility is one of the most profound sources of power that there is. It will change everything when you take responsibility for:

- ✓ *How you feel about others*
- ✓ *How you feel about yourself*
- ✓ *How you think*
- ✓ *The stories that you make up*
- ✓ *The meanings that you give things*
- ✓ *Your actions*
- ✓ *Your choices*
- ✓ *Your behaviors*
- ✓ *Your feelings*
- ✓ *Your words*
- ✓ *Your reactions to people, situations, and things*

These are all sources of power. They are yours for the taking when you step into accepting full responsibility for your life. The good, the bad, and the ugly in all that you do and all that you experience in life is precisely where your greatest power lies.

Unfortunately, somewhere along the way, we got it all twisted up. We have it backwards. Somewhere along the way we were conditioned into insecure patterns of handing our power away, and we came to call it "being humble." That so-called humility keeps you from owning the power of your epic feats. It prevents you from celebrating your progress and rewarding yourself for your accomplishments. It literally creates what I call Awesomeness Amnesia where you legit forget all of the amazing things you do.

Then, to top it all off, we have been conditioned to shame ourselves *and* others for being confident, as if being confident is somehow arrogant and or conceited. When someone owns her true beauty, magic, and light, when she shines bright and revels in the glory of her awesomeness and holds an epic level of pride and love for being herself, we are subconsciously conditioned to think to ourselves, *Who does she think she is?*

So, we stay small to escape the judgements of others. We avoid triggering others. We "stay humble." In actuality, what you may have been calling humility is really just downplaying your epicness. This is such a disservice to you and everyone around you. Such behavior sends a message that we should all play small, stay safe, and allow just enough space for "good enough." Be good—but, whatever you do, *don't be too much.* This is what we tell ourselves.

Pair that pattern with the fact that, at some point along the way, many of us have succumbed to an addiction to blame. We blame everything and everyone around us for the undesirable patterns at play in our lives. We blame others because we feel like powerless victims. We move through life as if these things are happening *to* us. We lie to ourselves and buy our own bullshit, telling ourselves and others that we have no ability to create change. We just accept the current reality with an "it is what it is" attitude. We complain endlessly but never take the action required to create real change.

It is time to awaken to the power of owning the responsibility of what is truly yours and handing back anything that is not yours. Once you know what is yours and what is not, you can give yourself permission to be confident without shaming yourself. Then and only then you can stop accidentally handing your power away and stop stealing other people's power.

But first, in order to understand why we have it all tangled up in the first place, it is important to know what may get in your way. There are blocks to truly embracing what is yours. If you want to outsmart the versions of your mind that will tell you to avoid responsibility like the plague, you must first understand these roadblocks and find a way around them.

WHY YOU AVOID POWER & RESPONSIBILITY LIKE THE PLAGUE

POWER QUOTE

Blaming our behavior on forces outside of ourselves is a way of avoiding responsibility.
James Redfield

In our society there is a common misunderstanding that taking "responsibility" for something is somehow the same thing as accepting the "fault" or "blame" for that thing. Given this understanding, why the hell would anyone ever want to take responsibility? Taking responsibility has been tied to elements that no one in his or her right mind would be excited to own.

Yet responsibility is neither fault nor blame. That's just some old BS definition that distracts you from owning your power. Responsibility is actually freedom. If you are a part of the problem, then you can be part of the solution.

Responsibility is the power to choose. Responsibility is the power to change the future, to rewrite history, and to put a stop to the undesired pattern loops that are repeating in your life. But first you must remove shame, blame, and fault energies from your definition of responsibility. When you do shift out of the old model of blame and shame, you will gain access to the power to choose to give yourself the freedom to respond on your own behalf and in alignment with your deepest truths and desires.

The first step in this process of shedding the old is bringing consciousness to the very reasons that your subconscious mind is getting in your way. We will explore your resistance to change, the inevitable shame you will bump into as you grow, and how you may be using confusion as a masterful tool of avoidance.

Take notes as you read through this section. Pay particularly close attention to which pieces have the most profound grip on you. This will allow you to bring subconscious shenanigans into the light and transmute darkness into a launchpad for epic growth and expansion.

Resistance to Change

Want to guess why you don't own your power and instead you avoid claiming all that can be found in the absolute goldmine of growth that comes when you take full responsibility for your life? Yep, change. Once you do the work to identify where you are a part of the problem, you can either go back to blatant denial of, settling for, and tolerating shitty behaviors. Or you can change.

You can choose to drift aimlessly, allowing problem patterns to recur again and again. Or you can power up and make a change. You can continue to make the same choices on a very familiar and comfortable autopilot repeat. Or you can change.

Will you choose change?

Once you acknowledge your own active participation in the things you are experiencing that are less than ideal, you officially leave the Land of Ignorance is Bliss. Once you have awareness there is no going back, no matter how much you wish you could, you begin to expand your world.

There is a cartoon picture that I saw circulating on social media that describes our resistance in such a hilarious and on-point way. It's a cartoon drawing with a split frame that shows the same room with the exact same people in it but with two different questions being asked. On the top of the first picture is the question, "Who wants change?" Everyone in the room raises their hands. Above the second frame is the question, "Who wants to change?" What do you think the response is?

Yep, zero hands raised.

We want change. We want the dream life. We want the dream love. But to actually have what we desire requires owning the responsibility for the good the bad and the ugly in our lives. And that kind of ownership requires a ton of courage and bravery. It demands radical honesty with yourself and others. It requires that we change.

Let me give you an example of what I mean. Let's say hypothetically that I have a "friend" who spent the first 30 years of her life feeling unlovable. As a result, that "friend" repeated an ongoing cycle of dating emotionally unavailable men. (Just so we are clear, by "friend," I mean me.) If that feeling of lack of worthiness was somehow society's fault, my parents' fault, the education system's fault, the fault of the emotionally unavailable men that I dated, and/or literally anyone else's fault but my own, then I get to completely avoid taking any kind of responsibility for any and all of my own actions.

Yay for blaming! WOO!

If I pass on the blame and responsibility for my actions, I'd get to stay in the Land of Endless Denial. If how I showed up in life was someone else's fault, then I never have to face myself. If it's someone else's fault, I don't have to change. I don't have to feel any feels. It's quite a brilliant strategy for "safety," if you think about it. And by safety, I mean absolute delusion and denial and a one-way ticket to a Victim Convention where plenty of other victims (I affectionately refer to these victims as Victimas and Victimos) are waiting to connect.

We will talk more about Victima and Victimo behavior in depth later. For now just know that a Victima Convention is one of convenience, where you can sit around all day and talk about how your mother, father, spouse, children, the education system, culture, political constructs, and society in general are somehow at fault or to blame for all of the pain you feel and for all the pain you have caused others. The best part is, you don't have to own your own decisions. You don't have to take responsibility for your words, choices, behaviors, and actions throughout your life, because somehow none of it is your "fault." Convenient, indeed!

Why the hell would I want to be responsible for dating emotionally unavailable men and avoiding dating the ones who would have made epic, lifelong adventure partners? Why the hell would I want to be responsible for feeling unlovable? Can I get an amen?!

If I shifted the way I defined responsibility from the old model of reverting to blame, fault, and shame and instead stepped into responsibility for being an epic power source for all the growth I crave, then I would have to let go of a whole lot of stories I created about others and about myself.

But those stories have been my comfort blanket of perceived safety. I'd have to admit that I was wrong in some ways. I would have to detach from the comfy bond I have with my Victima, who tells me that it is all happening to me.

If I said yes to a willingness to change, I'd have to accept that, in some way, I was an active participant in creating my circumstances. I'd have to learn to connect with people in new ways instead of the old ways of connecting wound to wound. I would have to let go of the attention and significance that I get from living in the pain of my stories.

I'd have to eat some heaping piles of humble pie.

If I got brave enough to own my own shit and then make changes, I would have to start feeling things I have masterfully suppressed and numbed for decades. Are you seeing why it is so much easier to remain in the Land of Ignorance is Bliss?

By easier, I mean you can pick up the shame carpet, sweep your pain underneath there, and completely ignore the growing mound of unresolved pain that has you running in circles and keeps you stuck. You get to blame others. You don't have to feel or change and grow!

Yeah, "easier-ish." Sure.

Through the years I have walked my own path to unlocking new possibilities for power. I have learned that numbing and avoiding, resorting to denial, and residing in the Land of Ignorance is Bliss is literally like sleepwalking through life. These choices are preventing you from any chance of truly living. If that's "easier" for you then, sure, keep lying to yourself. Buy your own BS. Call it "easier."

Yeah, sure. Easier.

Numbing yourself, distracting yourself, and convincing yourself that you are just "letting loose," "relaxing," or "treating yo-self" to a drink or pot, or to TV or junk food, as if the numbing is somehow good for you, is just a one-way ticket to the Land of Ignorance is Bliss where you don't need to be responsible for your life. Your prize is that you never get to live!

WOO!! If someone else is thinking for you or carving out the path you choose to follow and if at any point it happens to be "wrong" for you, then you have someone to blame! WOO!! It's pretty brilliant, eh?

If, however, you listen to your own internal guidance, if you trust yourself and own your intuition, if you listen to your desires and honor your vision of the path you want to follow and it doesn't work out, then who can you blame? No one. It makes perfect sense that we follow others' paths for our lives blindly. We do it to avoid pain. At least that's what your Ninja Mind believes it's doing.

Remember the Ninja Mind is the version of your mind that is programmed to keep you "safe" and therefore assassinates any and all attempts for you to actually change, because the only thing that is "safe" is the pain you already know and masterfully avoid. So blaming is safe. Thinking for yourself is not.

In truth, can you see how such a choice to blindly follow paths that others lay out for you, in your attempt to avoid pain, is actually outsourcing your own power and avoiding responsibility? Can you see with such logic how you're not even giving yourself permission to think for yourself?

You are refusing the opportunity to try things on for size. You are denying yourself the opportunity to experiment and learn for yourself. Following others' paths blindly and hiding from your true power leads to a life of what ifs and regrets. When you make this choice by not choosing to change, you sacrifice years of your life for moments of fulfillment. Is that what you want to consciously choose for yourself?

You may feel like you'd be lost if you didn't follow the path that you've been blindly following. Perhaps that familiar addiction to "how" comes in to haunt you. You may feel lost and confused.

TAKE YOUR POWER BACK!

Do you really feel as if you know who you are right now? Do you absolutely love the life you are living? Are you proud of who you show up as every single moment of every single day on the path you are currently on?

#powerfulAF

If, by chance, you are blindly following a path and it doesn't even feel good, it doesn't even light you up, and you're not even sure of who you are, isn't it also true that you are "lost" already? The very essence of who you are is lost. If you keep going in a direction that doesn't serve you, then you end up guaranteeing that you'll be lost forever.

But when you have the courage to go off path and find your own way, the worst thing that could happen is that you'll be lost. We've established you already are lost. So, in actuality, you have nothing to "lose" at all. At the very least, if you try something new, you'll be giving yourself some kind of chance to find a way that might actually allow you to love being you.

Just a thought.

POWER QUOTE

What if I fall? Oh, but darling, what if I fly?
Erin Hanson

Do You Have an Addiction to Certainty?

At the center of this avoidance of responsibility and power is the human addiction to certainty. Our subconscious minds would rather follow a path blindly, even one that leads to exhaustion, depletion, depression, and unhappiness or yields no true fulfillment, because it feeds the addictive pull towards familiarity and certainty. We subconsciously choose sabotage to ensure certainty. We avoid going off path and we avoid giving ourselves the potential to actualize our dreams, because that would mean entering into the unknown.

Yet, certainty is merely an illusion. It is false.

One illustration of this is Jim Carrey's story about his father, who gave up his dreams so that he could take the "safe" road. Carrey's father had followed the path of "certainty," working for the same company for years, doing a job that was not his dream. Then one day his father was laid off. As he looked at his father's experience, Jim Carrey had a realization. "If you can fail at what you don't love, you might as well try what you do love," he says. Carrey then followed his dreams. He gave himself full permission to pursue his passion for comedy.

This approach requires change.

That is precisely what this book is going to ask you to do: change. Change the way you think. Change the way you define Power. Change the way you define responsibility. Change the way you define what it means to truly live. This book will fundamentally challenge the ways you have lived your life up to this point and offer up a whole new path to Power. This path will completely rock your certainty boat.

This journey we are on will give you access to new levels of consciousness. It will change patterns you are currently stuck in, and it will give you the opportunity to shift out of the path you have blindly followed up to this point—you know, that old path that led you to dead ends in your pursuit of true fulfillment, true happiness, and true love. Well, dead ends no more! Buckle up baby. This new path of conscious creation will open you up to an epic and legendary existence.

From now on, I invite you to do this crazy thing called thinking for yourself. It's rebellious. It may cause you to lose friends. Family members may turn on you. People will think you have lost your damn mind. They will say you have gone mad and call you crazy. Still, maybe for the first time in your life, you will understand what true power actually is.

Shame Is One of the Sneakiest Pieces of All

There is so much shame that is tangled up in learning and so much mourning and regret that comes up as you learn new things. No one prepared me for the shame I was going to feel as I stepped into more and more consciousness, responsibility, and power. In the moments that I discovered profound Ahas that would forever and sustainably shift the trajectory of my life, I found myself drowning in shame. God, I wish I had known all of this sooner, so that when I bumped into it I would have realized that it was a normal part of the journey.

I wish I had not allowed my Ninja Mind to derail me when I came face to face with shame. Remember, the Ninja Mind's job is to assassinate any and all attempts to grow because growing means entering into the unknown and the unknown is not "safe." The only thing that is "safe" according to the Ninja Mind is staying rooted in the certainty of what is familiar—even if that familiarity brings pain. What a brilliant way to derail your growth by throwing you into a shame spiral that will keep you stuck.

As you learn new things and grow, you will experience the pain of shame over not knowing sooner what you now know. You will time travel back to all of the moments in the past that you didn't know any better. You will find yourself swirling with the regret of not knowing then what you know now and beat yourself up for not doing it "right" back then. You may become embarrassed or depressed, as if somehow you should have known at that time what you did not learn until the here and now.

At some point in all of this time traveling and swirling, you will land on shame, which will tell you that not only were you wrong then but you are also bad now. Shame will tell you that you, as a human being, are bad. This, of course, is total BS.

But shame is sneaky. It is a brilliant stall tactic used by your Ninja Mind to keep you stuck, and you need to know what to expect in order to keep it from paralyzing you. When the pain of shame becomes unbearable, you may find yourself defaulting to denial or experiencing the state of dissociation with reality as a means of numbing your grief or pain over past moments of not knowing.

POWER QUOTE
Do the best you can until you know better.
Then, when you know better, do better.
Maya Angelou

When you bump into those inevitable moments of shame's emergence, shift your focus. Celebrate knowing what you know now and look into the future to find all the ways you can commit to making new choices with what you now know. Focus on the excitement of getting to be an even more powerful version of you now that you know what you know. If shame is still gripping you and taking you under, call a friend. Tell your friend what you are experiencing.

TAKE YOUR POWER BACK!

Secrecy breeds shame. Talking about it out loud takes the power away from shame. It allows you to get back to you.

#powerfulAF

There is also shame that is tied to owning who you are. Shame in owning your darkness. Shame in owning your vulnerabilities. Shame in owning your fears. Yet, there is so much freedom in doing just that.

My mom always said, "Don't air your dirty laundry." Then, in my book *Epic Sexy You*, I gloriously rebelled and shared 351 pages of "dirty laundry" with the world. I faced my fears head on and shared my darkness and vulnerabilities generously with readers, so they could grow alongside me.

Although hiding was instinctual and the safe play back in the caveman days tens of thousands of years ago (so one could blend in and "survive" in the tribe and not get eaten by a tiger), my choice to let it all out was actually quite intuitive of me. It led me to the power of freedom and true thriving. Tens of thousands of years later, these updated options are now available to us! I shared it all and bared it all to the world. When I did, I literally set myself free.

Don't get me wrong. I freaked out before getting eyeballs on the first draft of the first book; but once it was out in the world and everyone had access to it, I let go. I let go of hiding. I let go of someone else's idea of how I should navigate life. For the first time ever, I let myself be truly seen. It changed my life. I stumbled across the profound experience of what true freedom is—the freedom to be me. I let go of all the shit I was hiding inside and I set myself free.

What are you hiding? Identify it and set yourself free.

TAKE YOUR POWER BACK!

Freedom is found in what is counter-instinctual and yet completely intuitive. Own it all, unapologetically. If you are hiding anything at all, you are not actually going to experience what true freedom is.

#powerfulAF

YOU MIGHT BE HANDING YOUR POWER AWAY LIKE A HOT POTATO

POWER QUOTE

The best years of your life are the ones in which you decide your problems are your own. You do not blame them on your mother, technology, or the president. You realize that you control your own destiny.

Albert Ellis

If you are avoiding responsibility for anything at all in your life, you are handing your power away like a hot potato. Sometimes handing power away is so damn sneaky that you don't even know you are doing it. It doesn't matter what someone else does or does not say or do. You get to consciously decide for yourself what you want, how you respond, and how you communicate. So stop handing your power away, yo!

How others react and respond is theirs, but how you show up in it all is all you boo. Again, it is easier-ish if how you show up, how you behave, how you tell the stories about what has happened, and how you feel is somehow not yours, because then you get to avoid having to change. This means you avoid feeling all the feels, such as the discomfort, grief, and shame that change inevitably brings. Easier-ish—if living an epic and legendary life isn't really your jam.

TAKE YOUR POWER BACK!

If you outsource the responsibility, then you will never have the true freedom to be you. When you outsource responsibility you will never actually live a fully awakened and powerful life.

#powerfulAF

Let's talk about some examples of what you are responsible for, so that the next time you catch yourself handing the gold that is your power away, you can take it back. You can own it and transmute that sneaky low vibe stuckness into forward movement.

POWER TRAP
Projecting Your Own Stories

Want to hear something that will be a game changer for you? You cannot make up a story about what someone else thinks or feels about you without that story somehow being a projection of your own beliefs about yourself. Somewhere deep inside of you, you believe the very stories that you are making up inside your head. Then you are conveniently saying that someone else was the author of those stories, so as to avoid being responsible for the pain and chaos that said stories are creating in your life.

Yeah, let that sink in. Then, consider:

✦ What are some of the **stories you are making up**? You know, the ones that are getting in the way of the very things you desire.

42

✦ If you are being honest with yourself, what are you doing to **feed the perpetuation** of those stories?

✦ What is it about those stories that you actually **believe to be true**?

✦ If you were to **give yourself permission** to write new and more empowering stories, what might they be?

✦ For the version of you who is able to believe the more empowering stories to be true, what are all of the **ways that you might show up differently** than the version of you who believed the old limiting beliefs?

Give yourself the gift of consciously writing a more empowered story. Then become the version of you who is in alignment with what you actually want to believe to be true!

POWER TRAP
The Blame Game

At the beginning of my power-awakening journey, when I was asked if I thought I was lovable and for the life of me I could not get the word "yes" to come out of my mouth, can you guess what one of my first questions was? Yep: *Whose fault is this?* It's my parents' fault. It's society's fault. It's the education system's fault.

Handing my power away like a hot potato.

If you are blaming anyone for anything at all in your life, you are handing your power away. For example, when I broke up with an ex, I wanted it to be all his fault so that I didn't have to feel all the feels. Yet, if it was all his responsibility that we didn't keep the relationship going, then I get no growth. When you play the victim and take no responsibility for your own life, you literally rob yourself of growth.

If there are any situations in your life where you feel like you're the victim and that it all happened to you and "poor you," stop.

If at any time you hear yourself say, "It's their fault because..." or "I did that because you..." (insert a whole list of justifications, excuses, and "reasons" for you to not own being an active participant of what happened in your own life), stop.

If at any point you hear yourself say, "I'm doing this because they..." (insert the reasons you are suggesting that your actions were somehow the direct result of someone else), stop.

If any of these ifs are at play in any situations in your life, then, for the love of unicorns and sparkles, can you please stop that crazy-making?

Take your power back by asking yourself how you are an active participant in whatever happened. Own what is yours, so you can take your damn power back.

No one is powerful enough to make you feel, do, or be anything unless you let them. Even if the radical honesty with yourself in those moments leads you to acknowledge that you are currently outsourcing your power, then acknowledge that to yourself too. That's the only way you'll stop the crazy train to the

Victima/o Convention, where no power exists for you whatsoever since you are ignorantly claiming to be at the effect of life.

POWER TRAP
Outsourcing Decisions, Desires, Actions, and Alignments

I constantly watch people hand their power over to Spirit or fate or destiny as opposed to owning their power and free will and knowing that all decisions in life are theirs and theirs only to make. *You* are responsible for knowing what it is that you want. *You* are responsible for being in alignment with what you want through your actions, your thoughts, your words, and your choices. And *you* are responsible for taking the action to consciously and consistently move you in the direction of your desires and dreams.

Every single day that responsibility rests only with you.

Outsourcing any of that responsibility to Spirit, God, the Universe, or fate is a sneaky way for you to get to sit back and do nothing. If you sit back and say, "Whatever is meant to be will be," then you are buying a whole heaping pile of BS from yourself.

TAKE YOUR POWER BACK!

---

*You are the
Master Creator
of your life.*

#powerfulAF

.

POWER TRAP
Gossiping and Complaining

Your energy is your power, and what an epic source of a zero return on investment of your energy gossiping is. If you catch yourself talking about someone else and it is not solution-oriented, but is instead simply talking about someone behind his or her back, you are handing your power away. You are also putting yourself in an energetic vibration that will attract a whole convention of Victimas and Victimos.

Your Victima/o may even lie to you and tell you that you are being solution-oriented and just momentarily talking to others in order to explore what you would like to do to resolve the issues you are facing with someone. While it is great to talk it out and explore how you feel before connecting with the person, if you find that days and weeks and months go by and you never actually have the conversation with the person directly, then let's not put lipstick on a pig. Let's call a spade a spade: you are gossiping and complaining.

I am telling you this because handing your power away is sneaky sneaky and you are worth so much more in life than merely being at the effect of your own self-limiting behavior. Give yourself the gift of forward movement and power. Speak directly to people with whom you have conflicts.

TAKE YOUR POWER BACK!

Choose to communicate and clarify
in lieu of gossiping and complaining
and your whole life will transform.

#powerfulAF

POWER TRAP
An Addiction to Busy

There is a pandemic in our society. As a society, we have bought in to an addiction to reacting to the world and whatever may be thrown at us in the course of any given day rather than responding responsibly. When you have an addiction to busy, your subconscious mind constantly seeks things to interact with or react to and you fail to consciously create your day.

Many of us have an addiction to reacting to life and handing all of our power away in the process. Are you always "too busy" to be proactive and move confidently in the direction that your heart and soul wants to go? When you take your power back, you will focus on investing your energy in things that Really Matter (RM).

If you find yourself incessantly checking your phone to see if someone has messaged you, checking your email every five minutes to see what needs your attention, and answering your phone every time it rings—even if you are in the middle of something else, because someone may need something from you, you may have an addiction to busy. If you check social media constantly to see what you can engage with and respond to, then you, my friend, are handing your power away like a hot potato.

The denial of the distraction is what gives more power to the Addiction to Busy. Once you identify your distractions, your awareness of them will allow you to start to take your power back and step into more and more conscious creating.

TAKE YOUR POWER BACK!

You are responsible for creating your own day.
You are responsible for what you focus on.
You are responsible for what you get done,
when you get it done by, and whether or not you
draw boundaries with your time. You decide
whether your time is a free-for-all of reacting to
the world of demands around you—or not.

#powerfulAF

POWER TRAP
Overgiving

If you find yourself surrounded by takers, consider this: the common denominator is you. If you find yourself feeling like you *give give give* and never get anything in return or if you feel unappreciated, then you get to ask yourself, "What is all of that overgiving all about?" If you are giving to others in hopes of receiving something in return and then resentful of others when they don't give you what you wanted, you are handing your power away like a hot potato.

Explore where in your life you are overgiving and get clear with yourself on why you are doing it. Play with how you might be able to take some of the energy you are pouring into the world outside of you and give it to yourself. Make it a top priority to clean up obligatory and/or strings-attached giving. Only give when you feel genuinely pulled to do so.

Other Common Power Traps

Here are a few of the other common power traps that could trip you up as you seek to master the power game.

✦ **Being problem-focused.** Focusing on problems instead of solutions. Focusing on what you and/or others are doing wrong instead of focusing on what you and others are doing right. Focusing on things you cannot control versus focusing on what you can change. Trying to control and/or manipulate others into change instead of focusing on yo-self. Take your power back by focusing on what you want to experience. *What do you want? What are all of the ways that you can be an active participant in creating what you want?* When you find yourself focused on problems, shift your attention to exploring any and all solutions that may be available to you in that given moment. When you catch yourself handing your power to someone else by trying to control and or change them, shift the focus back to you. Ask yourself what you can do to consciously create the shifts and change that you would like to experience. Remember, if you are not part of the problem then you cannot be part of the solution, and the only person that you can truly change is you. Invest your energy accordingly.

✦ **Asking others** what they think instead of thinking for yourself. Give yourself permission to take your power back. Go inside to check in with yourself. *What do you* *want? How do you feel? What do you need? What do you think? What are all of the possible solutions that are in alignment with the direction you want to go and grow in?* You have the answers within. Own that power the next time you are tempted to hand it away to someone else.

✦ **Being upset** with others for your own unhappiness, as if somehow how you feel is their responsibility. The only person who will ever have the true power to create sustainable happiness for you is *YOU*. Happiness is an inside job. If you are feeling less than in any way and you think it's someone else's fault, you're handing your power away. Take your power back by asking yourself, "How am I an active participant in this equation?"

✦ **Comparing yourself to others.** Please, for the love of unicorns and sparkles, can you stop comparing your first one hundred steps to someone else's one million steps? Focus on you. Allow where you are today to be your measuring stick for growth. Then, consciously take steps in the direction you want to go every day.

✦ **Competing with others** as if worth is a ranking system that tells you where you fit in comparison to the people around you. There is no competition. There is only one you in the world. You are unique and amazing. The best gift you can give to the entire universe is to just do you boo. What if, instead of competing with and comparing yourself to the world around you, you did this:

TAKE YOUR POWER BACK!

*If I were to let go of the rules and the boxes
that the world gave me, what might I create?
What else do I want to create? And what else?
You are here to create for the world, not compete
for your worth. You were born worthy. Now,
what would excite you and delight you
to create for this magical world?*

#powerfulAF

If at any point you find yourself handing away responsibility, you can take your power back by asking yourself:

✓ *How am I an active participant in this equation?*

✓ *What stories am I making up and projecting onto others?*

✓ *What is mine here that I am currently outsourcing?*

The answers to these questions will bring you back into your power. Every single time. If you are part of the problem, then you can be a part of the solution. Do yourself a favor and stop outsourcing what is actually yours. When you do this, watch out world, here you come!

TAKE YOUR POWER BACK!

Ask yourself what it is you really want.
If I were to create my wildly unique lane in life,
what might that look like?

#powerfulAF

STEALING POWER AND CALLING IT "LOVE"

POWER QUOTE

To rescue people from the natural consequences of their behavior is to render them powerless.
Henry Cloud

Oh boy, this one is super super sneaky. You may think you are "helping" others when in actuality you are robbing them of their own soul growth, doing the work for them, avoiding your own growth, and calling it all "love." Oy Vey!

One of the many creative ways that your Ninja Mind will keep you safe—aka locked into the familiarity of the known and therefore assassinating any and all attempts at expanding into more greatness—is that it will keep you busy. Your Ninja Mind will distract you, stall you, and convince you to avoid your own soul growth by stealing other people's power.

You'll find yourself doing other people's soul work for them and enabling the shit out of them. You may prevent them from taking full responsibility for their own life in the name of being "helpful." Not allowing another person to take full responsibility for their own life will keep you stuck. What you are really doing is avoiding your own growth, stealing their power, and contributing to their paralysis.

Let me give you an analogy that provides an incredibly powerful illustration of this. Are you familiar with the final stages of the process of metamorphosis for a butterfly? There is essentially a struggle that happens where the butterfly has to exit the cocoon through a super tiny hole. It has to fight to squeeze itself through the hole. As it does, it is actually squeezing out the remains of the fluid that is still in its newly formed wings. That process of struggle is a natural one that allows the butterfly to take the final step in preparing to fly.

If someone comes along and sees this emerging butterfly mid-struggle and cuts open the hole to "help" the butterfly so that it doesn't have to struggle anymore, that person is actually preventing the final process of the butterfly preparing its wings for flight. Instead of a butterfly, there will now be a life form that is stuck somewhere between a caterpillar and a butterfly. This creature will never get to fly, because it never got the opportunity to complete its metamorphosis due to the "helpful" person who felt responsible for its struggle and the discomfort they witnessed.

Consider these questions:

✦ How might you be **taking ownership** of someone else's struggle?

✦ How might you be **doing the work** for someone and robbing them of their growth?

✦ Where in your life might you be **thinking you are being "helpful"** when you may actually be stealing someone else's power and preventing them from their own process of metamorphosis?

✦ Where in your life are you **feeling responsible** for someone else's discomfort as they experience the shitshow that they themselves have created?

✦ What growth of your own are you **avoiding**? How are you stalling or distracting yourself from growth while deep in the weeds of "helping" others?

Up until this point, you were doing this Power Tangle from the subconscious and conditioned place of your mental programming. In all likelihood, you were not even aware you were doing it. As you come into greater consciousness and awareness, you will be triggered, but remember this: Triggers are gold! Triggers are the gateway to new possibilities.

TAKE YOUR POWER BACK!

There is power in choice. Consciously choose growth and humor over shame.

#powerfulAF

Once you know better, give yourself permission to do better, one step of awareness and one new choice at a time. Playfully practice identifying when you are subconsciously disempowering someone and calling it love. Then, take your power back as you ask and answer the following question.

TAKE YOUR POWER BACK!

If I were to give the gift of the struggle to this person and not interrupt their own process of metamorphosis, what might be the best-case scenario for them?

#powerfulAF

We often focus on what the worst-case scenario may be if we don't jump in to save the day. But what about the best-case scenario that might emerge from letting them fall? What might be the best thing that could happen for them? What might be all of the possible gifts of the struggle?

Remember all of your own moments of epic growth that were birthed in and through the struggle. Having those as vivid and visceral reference points will help you choose a new pattern the next time you see someone struggling and are tempted to jump in mid-metamorphosis.

The Line Between Enabling and Support

It is going to require heaping loads of radical honesty with yourself for you to accurately identify which side of the line you are falling on. Chances are, when you think you are being "helpful" and "supportive," you are actually enabling the other person to not do the work for themselves. You are inadvertently cutting short their own process of change because of your own discomfort at watching them struggle.

TAKE YOUR POWER BACK!

There is power in the struggle.
That power is theirs to own, not yours.

#powerfulAF

You are not responsible for another person's discomfort. If you feel like you are responsible and you are calling your intervention in their process "love," you are lying to yourself. Sometimes the best support you can offer is to let them sit in the discomfort that they themselves have created. Sometimes that is actually the most loving thing that you can do for them.

The fact that someone is not taking ownership for his or her own life and is a willing and active participant in allowing your enabling as a means of avoiding their own growth is that person's responsibility. You being an active participant in the enabling process is *your* responsibility. Responsibility is power.

You cannot change the other person, but you sure can change how you show up. You can become conscious of those occasions when you are enabling. You can change your behavior to allow them to have their own struggle in your presence. As an epic bonus, you will get back that energy that you used to endlessly give away to others.

WOO! What are you going to do with all that energy now? Perhaps focus on your own growth, eh?

The Fine Line Between Helping Others and Avoiding Soul Work

Whenever you find yourself super busy "helping" others and feeling responsible for their solutions, you are stealing their power and avoiding your own. Stop and consciously ask yourself, "What soul work of my own am I busy avoiding by focusing on everyone else?" If you are not keeping a close eye on that sneaky Ninja Mind of yours, it will lead you to believe that it is "easier" to feel responsible for other people's issues and problems and for their discomfort and pain than it is to sit still and be with your own.

This is because when you sit with your own issues and problems, you have to change. When you focus on your own growth, you have to navigate a minefield of shame and sort through that masterful confusion of yours that you use as a means of avoidance. That all takes work. So, yeah, your Ninja Mind will try to convince you that it is "easier" to avoid your growth and expansion and instead be "helpful" to others by offering them insights that are often not even in alignment for you. If they were in alignment you would be practicing what you preach; yet, you are often not doing that.

You tend to be too busy focusing on other people's growth to even notice that your Ninja Mind has you distracted, stalled, and avoiding your own growth. The cherry on top is that when you are "helping" others, you get to feel super good about yourself because you are calling the power-stealing "love." How convenient, eh?

Another clue that you are stealing another person's power is that you feel responsible for how they feel and/or what they do or do not do in their actions, behaviors, and reactions. For the love of unicorns and sparkles, stop stealing what is theirs. As an example, in the movie "A Star is Born," the father of the main female

58

character says that it is his fault that his daughter married an alcoholic because he was an alcoholic and that was what he showed her was normal when she was growing up. She looks at him and says, "You don't have that kind of power."

Boom. Mic Drop.

He was trying to steal her power without even consciously realizing it. That scene is a powerful illustration of what it looks like when someone has a root trigger which began in childhood. The temptation would be to blame the originator; yet, she consciously chooses to take responsibility for her own choices. The father's character is taking what isn't his. Yes, he may have wasted his own life, but he is not responsible for what she chooses to do with hers.

You are stealing someone's power if you feel responsible in any way for their happiness. That Ninja Mind will have you all sorts of twisted up, stalling your greatness at every chance it gets, avoiding your own soul work, and feeling as if somehow you get to be powerful if you can make someone who is miserable happy. Or, if you can get someone who is unhappy and not wanting a relationship to fall in love with you, then you're super powerful. Or if you help someone who is stuck get unstuck, then you are powerful.

Oh, God, no. This is called codependency, and it is what toxic relationships are built on. You deserve so much more magic and juicy living in your life. Feeling responsible for others will suck the life out of you. It will make you feel crazy. That is why we are doing this untangle.

Yay for sanity! Yay for powerfully conscious living!!

What Is Not Yours?

Here's a list of what's not yours boo:

✓ *How others feel*
✓ *How others think*
✓ *The stories they make up in their heads*
✓ *Their unspoken rules* *
✓ *Their happiness*
✓ *Their anger*
✓ *Their choices*
✓ *Their problems*
✓ *Their solutions*
✓ *Their struggle*
✓ *Their avoidance*
✓ *What they do and what they don't do*

* Whatever they believe you should or should not do, whatever they believe about who you should or should not be, even though they have yet to say a damn word to you about it. It's as if somehow you are supposed to read their mind and, when you do not, they would love for you to be responsible for that too. Nope. Not yours.

What Is Yours?

What *is* yours when you are communicating with someone else is the delivery. Are you telling the truth—the whole truth and not a half truth? Are you telling the raw real truth with courage and vulnerability, with love and compassion? All of that is yours.

What is *not* yours is how it is received once you do your part. Yet, we often spend so much time on how what we say may be received and/or rehearsing the five million ways it could go wrong. This is also known as stealing someone's power and focusing on what is actually theirs instead of investing your time in owning what is actually yours.

TAKE YOUR POWER BACK!

You are responsible for getting your truth out,
saying it out loud to the very person
you need to have the conversation with,
and doing it in the fullest expression
of truth with love and compassion.

#powerfulAF

I had someone say to me once when we were dating, "I'm afraid if we stayed together, I'd be a shell of a man." I was a little confused and asked, "Why is that?" He proceeded to share six month's worth of stuff that had been bothering him that he never brought up until that very moment. In an effort to hand him his power back, I told him that with that pattern of communication (six month's worth of dumping), no matter who he ended up with, he would be a shell of a man.

"You speaking your truth is yours, not mine," I told him.

He was a professional avoider of any and all confrontation, and he had convinced himself that his avoidance was somehow my responsibility. He was handing me way too much power. If I had actually felt responsible for how he was feeling, I may have accidentally stolen his power too.

Can I get an amen for the power untangle?

The art of not taking what is not yours is a journey. Give your loved ones the gift of handing them their power back when they hand you what is theirs. Come back to this section as needed to remind yourself what is not yours.

YOU ARE NOT A VICTIM; THE COMMON DENOMINATOR IS YOU

POWER QUOTE

*No one can make you feel inferior
without your consent.*
Eleanor Roosevelt

My own awakening into the depths of unshakable power that is available to us when we take responsibility came when I realized I had a pattern of dating emotionally unavailable or geographically unavailable, and often very toxic, men. I had dated a lot of toxic men, but apparently I had missed the clear signs of that blatantly obvious pattern. It seems the universe thought that I needed a brick upside my head.

So one day, just to make sure that the pattern became *super* obvious and crystal clear to me, I was gifted a relationship with a man who gladly had me take responsibility for all that was his. Nothing was ever his fault. Anything that he'd do that would cause a disruption in his own life he would very masterfully blame on everyone and everything around him. Many times that was me. Yay! He so fiercely believed in his own stories that I did too.

This was pre-awakening, y'all. I was in the thick of that Power Tangle! OK, let the crazy-making of the Power Tangle begin…

First, he told me that got injured at work. Then, with his newfound free time, he started "helping me" by staying at my place to keep my dog company while I was at work during the day. One day I came home from work to find that he had been real busy

63

that day moving all of his stuff into my apartment. Insert the look on my face of a wide-eyed WTF?

He didn't even acknowledge it when I got home. He was just sitting on the couch in his robe with his stuff everywhere. My second bedroom was now a storage unit for his things. To my recollection, we legit had no convo about it before he did it. I was deep in the weeds of the Power Tangle.

I said nothing because I thought that maybe I had done something to give him the impression that this was OK. My power was to say something, which I did not. I was avoiding my power. His decisions and his actions were his power, and yet I took responsibility for those.

Power tangle.

We would go grocery shopping together. I was picking up the tab for the food, and he would just start putting stuff in the cart. When I told him that we needed to cut back, because the grocery bills were triple what I used to spend when it was just me, he would look at me like I had killed his puppy. He would walk away and not speak to me for the rest of the time we were in the store.

Oh, and since we are all friends here, let me just tell on myself and be real damn honest. I would often feel bad and then put the stuff back in the cart.

First of all, can we talk about how I was paying for it all? Even though I knew damn well that my choice to continuously pick up the tab for everything was completely disintegrating any and all attraction that I had to him, I kept carrying the load. Now, don't get me wrong, I am all about partnership and, since I am abundant AF (As F*ck), I super enjoy sharing my wealth. Yet, I was literally paying for *everything* in our relationship—groceries, rent, toiletries, etc.—and he not only contributed zero monetarily, he also contributed zero around the house. He seemed to be turning more and more into a child than a man.

Looking back now I can see that I was an active participant in the pattern that led to the inevitable demise of the connection. To be clear and own my power here, no one was making me do anything. The overfunctioning was entirely my responsibility—even though at the time my Victima may have liked to claim and blame otherwise. However, back then, even when I saw the glaringly obvious pattern of my continual overfunctioning and its damaging side effects, I kept doing it anyway, because I didn't want to hurt his feelings. I was taking responsibility for his feelings instead of simply owning mine. I chose my own discomfort, avoiding his potential discomfort with the truth and hoping to set us up for love, connection, and chemistry.

Let me repeat that because I know I am not the only one who has experienced this flavor of the Power Tangle. My Ninja Mind—the part of the mind that wants to keep me small and comfy and therefore assassinates my greatness and any and all attempts to own my power—convinced me that I had to hide my true feelings, and overfunction on an ongoing basis, in order to get and keep love. What kind of crazy-making, ass-backwards crap is that? I avoided the discomfort of an honest raw real conversation in an attempt to be able to sustain the status quo of the love we had. Hello, Epic Power Tangle and buttloads of backwards thinking that actually led to me resenting myself for not saying anything and resenting him for not reading my mind.

Oy Vey!

I know now that avoidance always leads to resentment. Yet, my Ninja Mind, in its attempts to keep me safe, aka stuck, in the pain of all things familiar, kept me under the false illusion that avoidance was somehow protecting love. Do you see the crazy-making the Ninja Mind does if you aren't paying close attention? Just so we are super clear here, the reality is that avoidance demolishes any and all chance of love ever happening.

Second, let's address how I was conditioning him to throw temper tantrums every single time we went shopping. I would put shit back in the cart, even though I would act like a victim every time he put things in the cart. Um, hello, how am I an active participant in the perpetuation of this crazy train cycle?

You feel me?!

After two months of him not working and zero attempts on his part to find a job, I told him he needed to get a job and help out financially since I was paying for everything. He then told me that I was controlling and that I was acting like the man in the relationship. He said I was not supporting him and his dreams.

Yet again, I took responsibility for his feelings. At the same time, I totally ignored my own responsibility. I refused to own my desire and hold a firm line on what it was I wanted and needed. I started to think that maybe he was right. Maybe I was being too aggressive. Maybe asking for what I want and expressing my needs was somehow masculine. Maybe I should learn how to become more feminine.

Hahaha. Oh, the crazy-making of the Power Tangle. I dunno, maybe his dreams were to stay at home all day and watch movies in his robe. Dream big, yo.

Oh boy, this one is a deep rabbit hole of Power Tangle that I had gotten myself into. I even somehow felt responsible for him not working, so I gave him money for school, y'all. I was enabling the shit out of this man, and I was a total Power-Tangle Puppet.

Dance, Morgan, dance!

I was taking on the responsibility of his problems and his solutions. Then, when I would finally attempt to own what was actually mine by speaking up for myself, I quickly went back to the Power Tangle Dance. I started to feel as if maybe I *was* responsible for his happiness, after all, and I should just be a good woman—you know: shut up, be in denial, and tolerate his shit.

Be the cool girlfriend, Morgan. Why do you have to be so difficult, Morgan?

Baahaha. Oh man, I was so deep in the weeds!

If you are anywhere in here, or even experience a fraction of this crazy-making, this book will really help you illustrate all the sneaky ways the Power Tangle infiltrates your life so that you can finally know better and do better. It is high time to get busy living in your true power as opposed to handing it away, avoiding it, or stealing power that belongs to others. Woo!

OK, so after enough bricks upside my head and many many dances in the Power-Tangle Tango I finally broke up with the man-child and committed to reforming myself in an effort to prevent this from ever happening again.

For some reason, at first I thought I could reform my selection of men without the help of a therapist or life coach. I started reading books and trying to figure it all out myself. I truly thought I had gained epic traction on the relationship front when I started to date a new guy at the office who appeared to be genuinely kind, funny, smart, handsome, and charming.

He was younger than me; yet, he came right out of the gate saying he didn't want to play any games. If we were going to date, it would be exclusive, he said. Especially since we worked together. You know, so we could prevent any drama.

It was refreshing.

After about a month of dating, I was reflecting on how much I had grown. I was so proud of myself. At first I had been keeping our relationship a secret at work, just to make sure that it was going to be something solid before making it more known. One day, as I was out to dinner with one of my closest girlfriends from work (who happened to be in the same position as him), I decided to open up finally and get the inside scoop on my guy.

"Hey girl," I said. "Give me the scoop on the new guy."

Her response? Wait for it...

"I am kind of dating him." She said it in such a giddy and excited way, I literally could not hear anything else she said for a little while after that. This guy knew she and I were close friends. I had pictures of her framed around my house. This wasn't just a casual coworker or an acquaintance. She was someone I truly considered a friend. And he knew that.

When I finally told her I was seeing him, too, we realized that when he was telling me he was "busy," he was paying attention to her and vice versa. When I confronted him about it, he said he didn't remember us having the conversation of being exclusive.

I remember telling someone about what had happened and he said, "Sounds like an insecure guy that needed the validation of two beautiful women to make him feel like a man. He must have been super needy for that validation since he was going after two close friends in order to make himself feel good about his manhood."

Yes indeed.

This made me realize that this was yet another emotionally unavailable man that I had chosen to date. That undeniable fact helped me make one of the best decisions of my entire life. I hired a therapist to help me explore the recurring pattern. And then I hired a life coach to help me move forward into new possibilities.

These two experiences with Captain Super Insecure and the Man-Child were such blessings. They were the very catalysts for me to start to consciously explore what was going on underneath the surface. I started to realize that in the past every relationship would end because a man I was with was found to be cheating or lying or his addictions created too much destruction or the physical distance between us wasn't working anymore.

Each time, the primary questions for me were always:

✓ *What is wrong with him?*
✓ *Why would he do this to me?*
✓ *What is wrong with men?*

Oh boo to me. My bad, guys. I didn't know better at the time!

Ladies, if any of these questions are hanging around anywhere in your subconscious mind, you are going to be missing out on some epic and amazing men, so pay attention!

These ongoing experiences awakened me. They led me to face a pretty profound question that changed my life forever. I asked myself, "Is it true that every man on the planet is a liar, addict, and cheater? Is it true that all the good ones happen to live out of state?"

No. Of course not.

So then, is it possible that perhaps I am the common denominator in every single scenario? Perhaps I might consider the recurring patterns in my own life? Perhaps I could use a little help sorting out why I keep picking the emotionally and geographically unavailable men?

Yes. Oh, shit!

Radical honesty with the self and truth bombs for the win! As I began to embrace the notion that the common factor in every single scenario was always me, I started to shift into more and more of my power by asking myself three Conscious Power Questions—questions that could actually allow me to start to shift out of old patterns that no longer served me.

Those questions included:

✓ *How am I an active participant in this?*

✓ *What am I repeating in this cycle?*

✓ *What can I choose to do differently to make an actual shift and stop this pattern?*

When I started to ask myself these questions, again, I very quickly realized that ***the common denominator is always me.*** I began to realize that taking responsibility was the key to owning my power to change the future, to rewrite history, and to stop the undesired pattern loops from recurring.

So, let's explore what my parts to own were in this crazy-making pattern. For starters, I had to admit to myself the most glaringly obvious pattern: I was the one choosing emotionally unavailable and geographically unavailable men. No one else was doing that, that was all me!

When I dug deeper I realized that this was a masterful way of keeping myself "safe" from any potential rejection. If I chose people who were never going to truly be available, I would never truly be hurt. Tada! I would be "safe" as in never get to experience love. Safe. Yeah, sure.

Oh, the joys of the subconscious mind.

I began to realize that I clearly lived in denial in most relationships. This was the only way I was able to stay rooted in the "safety" of continuously choosing unavailable people, lying to myself that I wasn't doing that, and then playing the confused victim when the depths of their emotional availability would inevitably reveal itself. I tolerated shitty behaviors and I massively overgave.

When I became part of the problem, I was able to become part of the solution. I chose to change the only thing in the equation that I could control—me. I also uncovered a pattern where I was choosing who I would date while drunk.

Yep. I was masterfully avoiding truth and reality via my own personal favorite escapism portal of alcohol. Do you remember that picture of me from the beginning of the book? The Sleepwalker? Passed out? Yeah, so she was the one choosing the people I would date.

Hello! It was blatantly obvious to the whole damn world but me as to why I was the Captain of the Struggle Bus when it came to dating. Yet, I legitimately had no clue that drinking was a part of the problems I was experiencing in love or the lack thereof. Go figure! Haha!! That's what happens when you are really committed to denial and being besties with your Victima! Oops!

So guess what I did?

In taking responsibility I asked myself, "What decisions do I need to make and or which behaviors do I need to modify in order to align myself with the Epic Love I genuinely want to experience?" I made the decision to become an active participant in the solution instead of the problem, and I quit drinking. Six years sober.

And it all started with realizing this:

TAKE YOUR POWER BACK!

I am not a victim. The common denominator is always me.

#powerfulAF

I have not even come close to any kind of toxicity that I used to encounter continuously. Oh the joys of taking responsibility for one's self and becoming an active part of the solution! What I found was that once I removed the most predominant denial mechanism that I used to masterfully avoid reality, I was forced to face truth. I was forced to face myself. I was forced to face what was actually mine and then give myself the gift of change.

Acknowledging that I was an active participant in all of the crazy-making in my life set me free. It was the catalyst of my own epic metamorphosis. See what can happen when you embrace responsibility? It is your turn to lean in and embrace what is yours so that you can take your power back!

Power Play

Take out a pen and your journal so you can do a deep dive soul play that will lead you to more and more unshakable power!

✦ What are some **recurring patterns** in your own life that you would love to bring to a stop?

✦ What are all of the ways that you are being an **active participant** in that pattern?

✦ What are you **repeating in this cycle** that you can do differently?

✦ How can you make an actual shift and **stop the perpetuation** of the pattern?

✦ What do you actually **want to experience**?

✦ What new **decisions** do you need to make in order to shift this pattern towards what you truly desire to experience?

✦ What **behaviors** do you need to modify to align with your desired experiences?

✦ What are some of the most common **feelings** that you continuously experience that you would like to experience less of?

✦ What are all of the **things that *you* are doing** that are contributing to making you feel that way?

✦ What are some ways you might be able to shift **how you show up** so as to change the experience?

✦ What are the feelings you **want to feel more of**?

✦ How might you be able to be an **active participant** in creating those more desirable feelings?

Remember that you are never a victim. You are always the common denominator in everything that you experience in life. When you become a part of the problem you can become part of the solution.

TAKE YOUR POWER BACK!

Allow yourself to be an active participant in the creation of what you genuinely desire to experience and watch your entire life transform.

#powerfulAF

WHAT DOES IT LOOK LIKE WHEN YOU ARE OWNING YOUR POWER?

POWER QUOTE

The happiest people in the world are those who feel absolutely terrific about themselves, and this is a natural outgrowth of accepting total responsibility for every part of their life.
Brian Tracy

Now that you know what it looks like to steal other people's power and also to masterfully avoid your own by handing your power away like a hot potato, let's talk about what it actually looks like to own your power. This will give you some ideas for what you can play with to move you forward in the direction you want to grow in.

Clues That You Are Owning Your Power

✦ **You ask yourself powerful questions that walk you back into your power.** For example, if you don't feel as lovable or powerful as you would like ask yourself, "What are all of the things I am doing that are showing me that I don't feel like I am lovable or powerful?"

When I did this conscious exploration back in the toxic man era, I realized that I was super busy showing myself all the ways that I didn't feel worthy of an epic and legendary life and love. I was drinking to the point of blacking out on a rather regular basis, sleepwalking

75

through life, making poor choices and decisions about who I was allowing in my inner circle, tolerating super shitty behavior, overgiving, saying yes when I wanted to say no, saying no when I wanted to say yes, putting everyone else above me and leaving no room for me on my own priority list.

When I took responsibility for how I was feeling, I was able to become a part of the solution and change my behavior. I was finally able to align myself with the love, connection, and presence I truly craved.

You can play this question game with whatever you desire to feel more of in your life. Ask, *What are all of the things I am doing that are showing me that I don't feel like I am...?* Insert what you desire to feel and/or experience. And *What can I do to take my power back and align myself with what I truly want?*

✦ **You are radically honest with yourself about all the ways you are an active participant in everything you experience.** That radical honesty and ownership of responsibility will truly liberate you. It will set you free! If you are a part of the problem, then you can be part of the solution.

If, on the other hand, you decide to stay committed to being a Victima or Victimo, then you will likely refuse to accept any responsibility for your life and be stuck in a hamster wheel of hell, repeating every less than desirable pattern that you have currently in your life. So, you own your power by asking yourself:

How am I being an active participant in the less than desirable things I am experiencing? What are all of the possible ways that I can be an active participant in creating what I actually want?

✦ **When you are wrong, you own it.** Whether you said something that you are not proud of saying or did something you are not proud of doing, you own it. Perhaps you reacted in a way that you are not proud of, and now you acknowledge what you did that was not in the highest alignment with your best self. You consciously explore how you can do it differently next time.

   The true goldmine comes in you committing to putting that learning into action as you move forward. You realize that, by owning your actions, behaviors, and choices, that you are not bad; nor is something wrong with you. Rather, you understand the power that is available to you in owning what is yours so that you can stretch and learn and grow.

   When you do, you can choose a new way next time, so you can get to be proud of being you. There is a lot of power in not letting the ego get in the way of you owning what is yours.

✦ **You realize and own that you are one million percent responsible for how you feel.** You know that if you are seeking happiness outside of you, you will always feel less than. As such, you consciously ask questions that help walk you into more and more responsibility:

✓ *How are you being an active participant in whatever is creating the less-than-desirable feelings you are experiencing in your life?*

✓ *What are the feelings you want to feel more of and how might you be able to be an active participant in creating those?*

When you become the Master Creator of your feelings, thoughts, and actions, and you take responsibility for the good the bad and the ugly, you're actually able to start creating some really powerful things for yourself.

✦ **You celebrate yourself when you do something that moves you in the direction you want to go.** You give yourself permission to focus on what you are doing right and to reward yourself in ways that are in alignment with your goals rather than in direct opposition of them—like my old "treat yo-self" to a Benadryl and a bottle of wine reward! Oy vey!

You are well aware that if you do not consciously check in on your progress that you leave yourself wide open for Awesomeness Amnesia where you will conveniently forget all of your epic badassery. Then your Ninja Mind will convince you that you have put in a ton of work with no results so why bother?

To stay ahead of the Ninja Mind's shenanigans, you purposefully schedule calendar reminders to check in with yourself. You frequently look back at your progress, capture it, and see how far you've come. You are a badass!

✦ **You own compliments received with a resounding and excited "Thank you!"** And, if you do not feel worthy and or if you feel insecure, then you take the responsibility for that. You do the work to explore the root cause so you can heal and move forward in the direction you want to go.

✦ **If you are unhappy, you ask yourself how you are being an active participant in any and all patterns that are keeping you locked into repeating cycles.** You take a look at actions that create the feelings of unhappiness. Then, you take action to change what you can. You consciously own your responsibility for the creation of more happiness in your own life.

✦ **You know that life is happening _for_ you.** Whenever something goes a little wonky, you stop and ask yourself:

   ✓ *What is this trying to teach me?*

   ✓ *What is the lesson here?*

   ✓ *What are the blessings and gifts that this experience is offering me?*

✦ **You know that, in pursuing epic and legendary, you may in fact be "too much" for some people.** You acknowledge that those are most certainly *not* your people. Your people shine bright, pursue epic and legendary alongside you, and support and celebrate you as you expand. For everyone you trigger with that bright light that you are, you know that you are a gift to them if they so choose to accept it, for the trigger is merely an invitation to them to step into more of their own power.

✦ **You focus on possibilities, all day, every day, asking:**

    ✓ *What are all the possibilities available to me? And what else?*

    ✓ *What are all of the creative solutions I have access to in order to get what I want?*

✦ **You think for yourself.** You define things for yourself. You question everything. You give yourself permission to go internal and check in with how it all feels to you.

✦ **You are a conscious creator.** You are a proactive participant in your own growth, consciously exploring questions that will walk you into more expansion. You ask yourself questions like these:

    ✓ *When was the last time I tried something new?*

✓ *When was the last time I felt truly bold and courageous?*

✓ *When was the last time I looked at an undesired, recurring pattern and asked myself what a new option would look like and then tried the new way?*

✓ *What am I afraid of that would both terrify and exhilarate me, knowing that when I do that very thing I will have a new reference point of how badass and unstoppable I am?*

✦ **You consciously choose dreams over comfort.**

✦ **You take responsibility for what is yours.** You release others from being responsible for your life, even if they were a contributor to the root cause or the trigger. The cause may not be yours, but the healing sure is. Own it and set yourself free!

✦ **You do the work.** You let go of anything that is at all weighing you down or keeping you stuck in the past.

✦ **You speak up for yourself.**

✦ **When someone gives you an insight, opinion, or a piece of advice, you consciously check the source.** As Brené Brown puts it, "If you are not in the arena also getting your ass kicked, I'm not interested in your feedback." YESSS! Give yourself the gift of surrounding yourself with people who are in the arena of life, doing the work, facing their fears, and choosing their dreams over comfort and familiarity. Perfection is not required, but you bet your ass you had better be doing the work.

✦ **You invest in yourself by learning to set boundaries.** Boundaries are such an epic source of power that I am writing a whole book on this topic and have a group coaching program on it. Be sure to go to the website and drop your email at the bottom of the page to be in the know and receive info when each piece launches. Also check out the current running Magic Sparkle Boundaries programs at www.epicsexyyou.com.

✦ **You understand the difference between "knowing" from the logical headspace perspective versus the true knowing that comes from actually "doing it," because you are putting things into action.** You gift yourself the true knowingness that comes from actual integration of conscious action that yields epic soul growth and expansion. You lead, teach, and inspire by being it. Do you *know it* or are you *doing it*?

Whatever it is that you want to learn and do and be, are you actually aligning your actions to have you get to experience it or are you merely learning it in your head and convincing yourself that you "know" it? Are you trying to learn how to swim without getting in the metaphorical pool?

Consider the following questions to own your power even more and go deeper and deeper with this concept for yourself:

✓ *What are some areas of your own life where you are subconsciously playing the "do as I say not as I do" game?*

✓ *Where you are telling others what they should do but you haven't actually done it yourself and/or you are not currently doing it yourself?*

✓ *What are some areas of your life where you are trying to learn without getting in the metaphorical pool?*

✓ *What might it look like for you to be in the pool learning as opposed to sitting on the sidelines and staying with the hypotheticals?*

✓ *What are some areas of your life or specific scenarios where you could get an epic uplevel if you practiced what you preached?*

✓ *What would allow you to be in even more alignment with what you "know"? For example, you might "know" that you need to eat healthy in order to feel amazing, but you may not be doing it. Explore it. Get curious. What is that all about?*

✓ *What would it take to walk you from logical knowingness into the doing, so that you bring yourself into alignment with what you want to experience?*

✓ *What if you stopped talking the talk and started walking the walk?*

✓ *What if you showed people examples of paths to personal power by living an epic life and embracing legendary greatness?*

✓ *What might you do differently in order to lead by being and doing vs. merely telling?*

✦ **You make decisions.** If you've got the metaphorical fence up your ass and haven't made a decision yet, then you're wasting energy and potentially missing out on some epic and dope AF (as f*ck) opportunities and people that are coming your way. You make decisions, and then you give yourself permission to be all in.

You get excited and delighted AF (as f*ck) about the path you chose. You know that if you convince yourself you've made a decision but you keep looking back and wondering, "What if?" then you never truly made a decision in the first place. Take a moment to think about what decisions you need to make in your own life. You know that true power comes from consciously exploring where you have even more opportunities to practice what you preach and align your actions with your desires.

TAKE YOUR POWER BACK!

---

*What do you need to let go of
so that you can truly move forward?
What are all of the possible ways that you
could create some epic "excite and delight"
on this new path you're choosing
to move forward on?*

#powerfulAF

It all comes down to you taking responsibility for the good, the bad, and the ugly and doing the work to move you toward an epic and legendary life. You don't like where you are? Become the Master Creator of your life and create change.

The root of the true source of our power is in the very thing we most often hand away—our responsibility. Responsibility is power. Whatever you want, get creative on focusing on the solutions that are available to you and do the work!

Finally, remember that although the root of any given trigger point may not be your doing, healing yourself most certainly is *your* responsibility. Power is an inside job.

TAKE YOUR POWER BACK!

*How much are you willing to own
every single thing you experience in life?*

*How much are you willing to own
the responsibility for the good
the bad and the ugly?*

*Ownership is where your
true power source lies.*

#powerfulAF

POWER
SOURCES

POWER SOURCES

POWER QUOTE

Now is the time to take back your energy,
your power, and your peace.
Debbie Ford

Now that we have played with one of the most profound Power Sources—responsibility, it is time to explore the other game changers that will provide epic upgrades of consciousness and allow you to truly become the Master Creator of your world. This entire section is filled with Power Sources that will help you walk the bridge from the outside world to the inside world. This is where your true, juicy, magical power is waiting for you to reclaim it.

When you play in the mastery of these Power Sources you will finally get to be free. Free to be you. To really, truly *love* being you. To do what you want, when you want, how you want.

Everything we are going to play with in this section is something that you can come back to over and over again as a playground and treasure chest of soul growth and expansion.

Here are the Power Sources coming your way:

POWER SOURCES

- ✦ Avatars and the Power of Who
- ✦ Power of Tribe
- ✦ Desire, Commitment, and Alignment
- ✦ Imagination—A Conduit to Infinite Possibility
- ✦ The Alchemy of Fear—Transmute Fear into Power
- ✦ Become a Badass at Failure & Persistence

- ✦ Be a Boss of Time
- ✦ The Truth Vortex

POWER SOURCE #1

AVATARS AND THE POWER OF WHO

POWER QUOTE

*Every next level of your life
will demand a new version of you.*

Unknown

One of the greatest pandemics of this world is the addiction to "How." It's like the whole world is on a hunt for the perfect 30-second, magic bullet solution to *how* to gain and sustain power and whatever else it is that you may crave—love, health, wealth, happiness, fulfillment, abundance, riches, energy, vitality, etc. If it takes more than 30 seconds to accomplish the how, most of us become overwhelmed, frustrated, and depressed. We start looking for someone to blame for how we feel.

OK, OK, let's be more generous.

Perhaps your threshold of tolerance for the transition period of growth is more than 30 seconds. Yet, when you hit your own personal threshold, you will inevitably bump into that good ol' "Why Bother" chatter in your head. That chatter makes you feel like you're spinning your wheels and nothing is working. You start believing you "must not be doing it right." You start to feel perpetually stuck.

At some point you come to grips with the fact that your current strategy isn't working. Which leaves you with the burning question, "What do I do next?"

This is the point at which most people succumb to the subconsciously inherited societal pattern of looking for another *How*. You start seeking another strategy of how to get you from point A (Stucksville) to point B (wherever you truly desire to be). Changing your how doesn't take into consideration the intentions that are driving your strategy.

Just like my boy Albert Einstein says, "We cannot solve our problems with the same thinking we used when we created them." And I would add a layer to that—a layer that seems to be missing in the consciousness of today's mainstream society: you cannot use the same WHO to try and come up with solutions when that particular WHO is the very one responsible for your current "solution" (aka your current problem, aka you living in Stucksville). Can I get an Amen?

It is not the HOW that is getting in your way it is the WHO. It is not the strategy, but the Who you are showing up as you apply and integrate the how that is your biggest opportunity for a massive, game changing uplevel. I am going to repeat that because it's a biggie and it is an epic game changer in being able to radically transform the amount of true power and fulfillment and happiness and confidence and success and self love that you can experience and sustain in your life.

TAKE YOUR POWER BACK!

*It is not the HOW
that is getting in your way.
It is the WHO.*

#powerfulAF

It is *Who* you are showing up as—*Who* you identify yourself to be—that makes the real difference. It is your thoughts and beliefs that are driving you. It is the intentions you set and the energy that is a part of who you are that allows you to perform the how.

There are literally an infinite number of ways that you can arrive at any given destination of desire. You will never be in shortage of a how. Ever. Your mind may try to convince you that you literally do not know how and that if you did know how you'd already be doing it. Yet there are endless hows that are available to you in this world, and a part of you knows that.

If this juxtaposition of beliefs is not something you consciously explore, you will circle around and around. You will chase your tail endlessly and blame it on the strategy time and time again instead of anchoring in where your true Power Source is. Your true power is always in owning and creating your Who.

Epic kudos to you for choosing to pick up this book so that you will not be among the majority of those in society, stuck in the never-ending trap of seeking endless strategies and hows that are found in the world outside of you. Your answers are waiting for you within.

This section is going to help you sort out Who you need to be in order to finally have what you want. You will find that the best you is going to be different in every scenario you encounter. I'll share some playful and humorous ways to identify which versions of you may be wreaking some havoc in your life and getting in your way. You will see that there are many Whos that you already have that you may not even consciously realize.

If you read my first book—*Epic Sexy You: No Limits. No Rules.*—or listened to the audiobook, you will remember a section where I introduced the concept of Avatars. In this book we'll expand on this concept in depth as it is one of the most foundational Power Sources that exists. Avatars are essentially the different Whos that you show up as in any given moment. Notice that the words Avatar and Who are used interchangeably as we explore this epic power source.

The amount of Power that you have access to is contingent upon your level and depth of consciousness. As Lao Tzu said, "The key to growth is the introduction to higher dimensions of consciousness into our awareness."

Amen, Lao, Amen!

And that is precisely what we are going to do right now: upgrade to a whole new level of capability and new layers of possibility. This expanded capability will free you to move toward whatever it is that you are craving to experience, to have, to create, to be, and to explore in this world. It all starts with your own awareness of and connection to your Who.

If you are not consciously creating your Who, you will be missing out on one of the most profound sources of power available to you. We are multi-faceted beings, and we play many characters in the course of any given day. It is time to give more awareness to Who is showing up each day. First up, we will play with Who is getting in your way.

You will notice that as you shift from the How to the Who, you will stop focusing so much on trying to change and control the outside world. You will naturally gravitate toward where the most epic shift available to you lies—*inside you*. You are the only thing you truly have the power to change, and consciously shifting your Who is an epic gateway to new possibilities.

How to Use This Power Source Section

✦ As you read about each of the Avatars, empower yourself to **change the names** to whatever feels most relevant and playful to you. Pay attention to what is hitting home for you. Use my examples as a mirror to see yourself in. Start to get to know which Who is getting in your way.

✦ You will notice I name and talk about my Avatars in the feminine. If you prefer to **name your Avatars** in the masculine, feel free to do so. I am merely using feminine language as that was what felt on point for me as I went through my own creation process.

✦ You are responsible for taking ownership of Who you are in every moment of your life. This entire Who exploration is all about **awareness**. That awareness is achieved as you explore consciousness-raising questions that will move you forward into more and more power, love, happiness, health, wealth, and everything else that you crave! Take your time to answer all of the questions you encounter. The more you explore the more you'll expand.

✦ *Get playful. Be Curious.* Find yourself in my stories. Laugh at me. Laugh with me. Laugh at yourself. There is so much power in **choosing humor over shame**.

✦ Once you are armed with an upgraded consciousness, you will have more choices in life when you feel stuck. You can begin to ask yourself:

✓ *Who is driving the car?*

✓ *Who is the captain of the ship?*

✓ *Who is running the show?*

✓ *Who might be a more powerful version of me to leverage in this moment?*

✓ *Who can take the wheel and be in even greater alignment with what I crave to experience in this moment?*

Avatars Getting in Your Way

There are a few Avatars that are pretty universal. These low vibration Whos might be getting in your way and you don't even know it. Let's bring the spotlight of consciousness to them so these sneaky sneaky, power avoiding, power stealing Avatars have nowhere left to hide.

Please know that you are not bad when you are experiencing these lower vibration Whos. You just have more options available to you that will allow you to access even more power and forward movement than these. Before we can access and create even higher versions of Whos, we need to gain awareness of the Avatars that are most commonly getting in your way.

When you can identify your Whos when they come up and have the tools you need to shift out of them, you pave the way into the creation of new options and possibilities.

AVATAR PROFILE
Victima / Victimo

Why is this happening to me??!
Whyyyy??! Poor, pitiful me!

This one is hands down the most common, sneaky and ruthless, power robbing Avatar of all time. Not only does this version of you hand your power away, you legit have access to zero power when you are experiencing this version of you. When you are in Victima, you are convinced that anything and everything is somehow someone else's fault. You'll feel like everything is happening *to* you. In this Avatar, you are associating responsibility with fault and blame and you are handing your power away like a hot potato!

When you are experiencing Victima / Victimo, you'll notice your significance is being derived in the pain and victimhood of your story. You may find yourself telling the same story over and over and over again. And the story is always about how it's all happening *to* you. Poor you.

You'll be avoiding confrontation at all costs and talking to every single person about the problem, all the while avoiding the very person who you have the problem with. Or, if you do say something to the person directly, it is often done through complaining or passive-aggressively stating all the reasons that you feel it is all their fault. Let me remind you that if you do not acknowledge you are part of the problem, then you cannot be a part of the solution.

When you are experiencing Victima / Victimo, the connections made in relationships with others are typically made victim to victim and wound to wound. As in, "OMG, that is awful; yes, that person is such a jerk! Poor you." You then proceed to share a story where you are a victim and they get to make you feel better. You're both championing one another's victimness, and both of you keep handing your power away. You stay there in Victimville together, endlessly swapping victim stories in your never-ending victimized way of moving through life.

Victima/Victimo is pretty predictable. When someone else draws a boundary or tries to hand Victima her power back, she goes into even bigger victim mode. Victima likes to recruit others to join in her story, so she will feel validated. Please hear this: *a Victima cannot be a victim without someone else allowing her to be so.*

Victima / Victimo wears blinders. She prefers denial and does not like the truth. Victima can make excuses for days on end. She's a chronic blamer. She often holds things in or at the least does not share what she is feeling directly with the person with whom she is upset. Instead, she complains to literally anyone and everyone who will listen, typically for extended periods of time.

If she cannot find someone to listen to her complaints, she will literally explode. To be clear, she doesn't explode because no one is listening. She explodes because she wants the person that she feels victimized by to know what a jerk they are.

At some point Victima will explode and dump on the person they are feeling victim to. For some Victimas it takes days, weeks, months, years, and or even decades later, but mark my words eventually she will explode. By the time Victima does finally say something directly to someone she has issues with, it is usually to let them know that they did a bazillion things wrong and that it's too late to create solutions. Oh yeah, and it's all their fault.

Then Victima convinces herself that she is being "courageous" and "speaking up" for herself, super empowered-like, when really it was just loads of time spent being cowardly and not saying a single thing, often pretending everything was fine while complaining to others about it. Victima has taken zero responsibility for the demise of something that otherwise could have been salvaged had she just spoken up.

Oy Vey, Victima. Oy Vey!

What Victima is sharing often comes as a surprise to the receiver. At the very least the receiver is left perplexed about how it is *all* their fault, since Victima legit never had a direct conversation with the person until now and Victima has made it clear that it's actually too late to co-create resolve. Still, Victima wants the other person to know that the end is here and it's all their fault. Victima takes *zero* responsibility for the entire duration of time that has passed where her unspoken boundaries have been violated.

As you can see, Victima would like for others to read her mind. If they don't, she will get very creative and find ways to blame them for her not expressing what she wants and needs. Victima outsources power likes it's her J-O-B.

SPOTLIGHT STORY

Let me be generous with my own Victima-ness and tell you a little story to help you find pieces of yourself that may be hiding beneath the surface for you. Feel free to laugh with me or at me. Either way, you are winning and learning, and we all win that way.

So, let's rock!

Once upon a time, I was in a relationship with a man who I loved very much. As we grew in different directions, things started to unravel. When we finally decided to part ways, Victima got busy straight away, throwing the most epic pity party of all time.

Victima wanted to know: *Why are you doing this to me? Why are you abandoning me?*

Um, just so we're clear, *I* was initiating the breakup as it genuinely was best for both of us to go our own ways. Yet Victima blamed it *all* on him. *Everything.* She kept saying: *He is abandoning me. He doesn't care about me. If he cared about me, he would want the same things as me. If he loved me, he wouldn't let me go.* Oh, and my favorite, quite laughable one was this: *He will be miserable without me. That will show him!* Oh, Victima.

In order to walk myself out of the Victima hole of Blame Shame Denial I played a little game with myself that I call, "The truth is: I was an active participant..." This is where I face the truths that I do not want to say out loud, and I own what is actually mine in all of this. This is where truth is an epic conduit to take your power back.

When you find yourself in an epic sense of denial that you have anything to do with the unraveling of your own life, you are literally handing all of your power away. You are choosing to live in Stucksville. This game will help you take your power back. Let me show you how this showed up in my real life example of the demise of our relationship.

The Truth Is: I Was an Active Participant

✦ *The truth is...* I had grown into a new version of me and was no longer who I was when we first started dating. I was the one who had changed. When we first started dating, I didn't want to get married and I required a level of independence that prevented me from true depth of commitment and intimacy.

We were completely on the same page at the beginning. We were in alignment. Then, about a year and a half into the relationship, I changed my mind. I decided I wanted a lifelong adventure. I decided I wanted to build a life with someone, to build a home with someone, to embrace a lifetime commitment.

I had completely shifted my desires and done a total 180. Yet, here I was feeling like the victim, as if he was the one who had changed, as if somehow he had blindsided me. When the truth was, I was the one who changed. I was putting him in a space where either he would have to change to come with me into this new vision I had created or he'd stay in the same place where we had started. After significant time and exploration, he chose to stay in the same place where we had started and it led to an inevitable gap that left us no longer in alignment.

There is a power that resides in choice. I am responsible for my choices. I chose growth. I chose to allow us to unravel since we were no longer in alignment. It was a choice. I am not a victim. *I was most certainly an active participant* in the unraveling of alignment. The truth is that wanting different things didn't make either of us right or wrong; it just meant we were not in alignment to continue on a shared path together. I chose to have faith in true alignment by clearing what was no longer aligned to make space for what is.

✦ *The truth is…* I chose resentment over discomfort enough times that I began to resent him and myself. What I mean by that is I avoided being uncomfortable via raw real honest conversations. Instead I had many conversations with him in my head that should have been spoken out loud. There were things that I was hurt about that we never fully processed together. I was afraid that if I brought it up it would be too uncomfortable or would perhaps contribute to the deterioration of our connection. The irony was that keeping things bottled up inside to prevent any discomfort led to my resentment of him and myself. And the relationship deteriorated anyway. I own that. *I was an active participant.* I learned the importance of radical honesty with the intention of love so the connection can stay strong.

✦ *The truth is...* I caught myself shrinking so as not to trigger him. That's one hundred percent my part. I own that completely now. I am an epic force to be reckoned with. I am a lightworker. I dream huge AF (as f*ck) and I manifest magic like it's my jam. Instead of owning all of my majesty and glory and truths, I made up stories that he would be triggered by my epic growth and epic light and epic soul power. I tried not to be too big around him.

How convenient that I blamed him for me hiding my soul magic, eh? I could have stayed in my power and radiance. I could have played huge, but the truth is I didn't. I contorted to fit myself into my own made up stories and limiting beliefs of who I thought I needed to be in order to sustain love and connection, which eventually led to me resenting him and myself. *I was an active participant* in the demise of our relationship by not fully owning my power, my magic, my truth, and my light.

✦ ***The truth is…*** I fell prey to the power trap of comfort. I wanted romance, but I wanted him to create it while I laid on the couch. Bahahaha. YES!!! And I was mad at him that he would have the audacity to be so damn lazy next to me. You hear that Victima blame game shenanigans?! Um hello, I was a comfy slob right there next to him, you dig?

The truth is I stopped showing up consciously. We'd spend night after night on the couch watching a movie, mindlessly numbing instead of consciously creating moments of connection exploration and love. Don't get me wrong. We had moments of co-creating consciously, but eventually the Power Trap of comfort took up more and more space.

I knew the importance of co-creating experiences and memories that would strengthen our relationship connection and our bond and I was not being an ongoing active participant in creating what I wanted. And how convenient that somehow it must be all his fault, eh? Sneaky sneaky Victima.

My Victima secretly wanted Epic Love without having to put the work in. The truth is I stopped being a conscious creator in our relationship. In reflecting on this truth, it was an epic lesson learned. I have learned to find creative ways to strive to keep the consciousness alive in all that I do. ***I was absolutely an active participant*** in the demise of our relationship.

A key to Power is owning what is yours and being radically honest with yourself about what the truth *actually* is. If you do this one thing, you can learn and grow from every single thing in your life. It genuinely is all happening *for* you, and if you are letting your Victima / Victimo run the show in any area of your life you are going to be stuck chasing your tail.

Find the courage within to face your own truths. Then, apply them consciously as you move forward in your life. Boom, truth bomb yo-self and set yo-self free! You may be thinking, "What about when I really am a victim of something?"

To which the response is as follows:

TAKE YOUR POWER BACK!

The root of the pain may not be yours,
but the responsibility of healing it is yours.
How much time you let it take
from you is yours too.

#powerfulAF

Victima will allow you to go your whole life holding onto one trauma point and blaming others for all the years you wasted. The moment that was taken by the original point of trauma or trigger may not be your responsibility, but every minute you let it take from you after that is yours.

Remember, with ownership comes power. You deserve to live the most expansive, majestic life of all time, but this is impossible when you are experiencing Victima / Victimo at the effect of life syndrome. When you are an active participant in the problem, you can be an active participant in the solution. Find the roots of your participation, and you will set yourself free.

Take your power back. You are so worth it.

Power Play

Ok, now it is time to roll up your sleeves and get to taking your power back! Get out a journal and pen and get ready to write out your answers as you explore a whole new level and layer of self mastery. This Avatar is legitimately handing ALL of your power away—to other people, to life circumstances, to literally anything or anyone you blame for how you feel. Let's find out where this Who is showing up so you can take your power back!

What are all of the areas of your life, your circumstances, your relationships, and your experiences where your Victima / Victimo may be showing up? For each area you identify, explore:

✦ What is this **trying to teach you**?

✦ Why might this be **happening for you**?

✦ If you were to consciously choose to **stop being a victim**, how might you like to show up instead?

✦ If you were to **give up playing the Victim** role in this area of your life, what possibilities might that free up for you?

✦ What might **taking your power back** in this area of life look like?

105

✦ How are you an **active participant** in the pattern?

✦ What are the **truths you need to face** to set yourself free?

✦ Knowing what you know now, how might you **do things differently** next time?

Also explore the following questions to get out ahead of Victima / Victimo. Digging deep here will help you move forward and shift out of this low vibe Avatar when she emerges.

✦ How might life in general be different if you stopped **being a victim**? How might you show up differently?

✦ What are the **trauma points** in your life where you are still blaming others? It's time to take your power back and seek help so you can finally heal. Consider all the possible ways that you can seek help to heal. Typically, therapy is an epic resource for helping heal deep trigger wounds and trauma.

✦ What is going on in your life that **feels shitty**? What are all of the ways that you are being an active participant in the perpetuation of that shittiness? Take your power back! How might you show up and become an active participant in shifting the experience into more of what you want?

✦ Where are you **settling for less** than what you want and complaining about it? Where are you making excuses for why it is the way it is? How are you an active participant in the settling? Get radically honest with yourself. What is the truth that you do not want to say out loud? Say that shit out loud. The truth will piss you off, and then it will set you free! Set yourself free. Then find something new that you can commit to—something that will create more of what you actually desire.

✦ What do you find yourself **complaining** about over and over and over and over? How are you an active participant in perpetuating your experience?

✦ Understanding you cannot change others and that your true power lies in changing things you can control {i.e. you}, what are some things you might be able to **do differently**?

✦ What would help shift **undesirable patterns** you are experiencing?

If you find yourself telling the same story over and over again, or complaining about the same person in your life over and over again, it's time to get real with yourself, take your power back, and try something different! Like my boy Einstein says: "The definition of insanity is doing the same thing over and over again, and expecting different results."

Break the crazy train cycle! You have the power to shift you. Do that, and stop focusing on what you want everyone else to change. Focusing on something you cannot change {i.e. others} is such a waste of life. You are so much more powerful than that. You deserve to experience so much more. Focus on you.

When you catch yourself being Victima / Victimo, remind yourself: "I am handing ALL of my power away; yo, not cool. Let's take it back! Where and how am I an active participant in this?" Set yourself free!

When dealing with a Victima / Victimo, you may find yourself thinking, "Maybe this is all my fault?" If this happens to you, let me just remind you that you are not that powerful. It takes two to tango, so you can stop and ask yourself:

✓ *What is actually mine here? And what actually belongs to the other person or group of people?*

✓ *Remind them that they are handing you all of their power and ask them how they are an active participant in the current situation.*

They may not actually own any of their shit in that moment (or maybe even ever), but at least you're drawing an energetic boundary, which you have now verbalized. This will allow you to get out of the crazy-making and untangle the power confusion.

Focus on the possibilities for all the avenues for moving forward and get creative with solutions you might like to play with to create something new. Remember that Victima / Victimo focuses on the problem, so when you want out of powerlessness you can take your power back by shifting your energy and attention to possibilities and solutions. When you discover where you have been an active participant in the perpetuation of the undesirable cycles, that is where your true power source exists.

Take your power back! Get a grip on Victima / Victimo!

AVATAR PROFILE

Spicy McChicken

I am angry, and it's all your fault.

The origin of the name of this Avatar may not be as obvious as the others I share. This one was actually a personal nickname that I was given in my 20s without me ever even knowing it. When I was 30 years old, I reconnected with a friend who ran in the same circle as me when I was in my early 20s.

When he found out that I had made the decision to be sober and that I worked with a therapist and a life coach to help me sort out all of my anger issues, he laughed. He told me that when we were younger I was such a fireball that, around the time McDonald's came out with the Spicy McChicken sandwich, he changed my name in his phone to Spicy McChicken.

All these years later, that was still how my name and number were programmed into his phone. Hahaha! I would love to tell you that Spicy is long gone, but the truth is that she is my inner child and she is still alive and well within me. Consciousness has helped me tame her from being the main Who in my life, yet I still need to keep an eye out for her so she doesn't slip in through the back door when I'm not looking.

Spicy's source of significance is derived in protection and fierce independence, even at the expense of her desire to experience love and connection. Common thoughts and phrases for Spicy include the following: "I can to do it myself," "I do not need anything from you," and, sure as shit, "Do not tell me what to do!"

In fact, whatever you tell Spicy to do, she will want to do the opposite, typically out of spite and even if that means she loses.

As a child Spicy had no problem getting grounded (rather continuously) to prove her point: "Your rules are dumb. I shall happily go to my room now and have no friends over for a week and have no phone access and no TV and no music. I don't care. Take what you want, but you will not take my power, and you sure as shit will not break me. Bring it on."

Sure, sacrificing freedom, friends, and time makes no sense in the grand scheme of things. But to Spicy it makes perfect sense, because the primary concern for her is to not let anyone take any of her power away. She is on the defense at all times, ready to *protect protect protect*, guard up, and fight if need be.

Spicy's emotional home is anger. When Spicy is asked to sacrifice in any way, she feels an epic sense of crazy-making injustice and then focuses on that injustice in an all-consuming way. Spicy is not the best at allocating energy. She genuinely thinks she is protecting her power so that no one can take it from her. Truth is, she is hoarding it. This is a clue that the energies of lack and fear are present.

And, boy oh boy, is Spicy angry. She looks for reasons to be angry, and she wants it to be someone else's fault that she is angry. She is handing her power away like a hot potato, making others responsible for her anger.

OY VEY!

If she tells someone no and they don't honor it, she is angry. She feels that others are responsible for having the same "common sense" as she does. She expects others to read her mind and know what she knows (or thinks she knows). She expects the other person to share the exact same experience, perception, and expertise as she does. She expects them to know whatever it is that she wants and feels and needs without her having to actually say it out loud to the person from whom she wants or needs things. Spicy feels that others should do x, y, z, a, b, c and/or whatever she thinks they should do.

Do you see Spicy's pattern? Do you see that she has a lot of expectation about how others *should* be? Instead of acknowledging who someone actually is and how a situation *actually* is, she thinks it should be different and she is pissed. Do you see how Spicy is very creative in finding ways to be angry and for it to be other people's fault?

SPOTLIGHT STORY

Let me share a story to illustrate this point. At the very beginning of my journey of awakening, I went on a spiritual trip to Sedona. I took off work for the first time in four years with the intention of disconnecting from the world. I wanted to consciously connect to myself. One day, I was getting ready in the bathroom while waiting for a spiritual practitioner to arrive at the house. About 10 minutes before she was scheduled to arrive I heard a car pull into the driveway.

What do you think Spicy's first thought was? It was, "What the hell is wrong with this woman? That is so rude for her to be 10 minutes early. I am not even ready yet. So thoughtless."

Spicy went to the door fuming and ready to *show* this woman how upset I was and how rude she was. Spicy was going to inform her that I am not ready and it is all her fault, so she would have to wait. When I opened the door, no one was there. Turned out that someone was just using the driveway to turn around. So I laughed at my Spicy and went back to getting ready.

Then the time came for her to be here and she had not arrived. A minute past our agreed-upon time and Spicy was back, ready to be helpful, thinking of all of the ways she was going to be mad at this woman for wasting my time and making me wait. Long story short, things had gotten lost in translation, and the practitioner thought I was coming to her.

Of course, Spicy had a lot of opinions about the company I used to set up the meeting and the fact that they had dropped the ball on the communication. By the time she arrived an hour after our agreed-upon start time, Spicy was so excited to have so many things to be upset about. She was like, "I got you girl!"

Defenses up. *Protect protect protect.* On guard!

When the woman arrived, she could feel my anger. Spicy does not have a good poker face. You'll always know where you stand with her, because it is made pretty damn obvious. It quickly became clear that I was not the first Spicy McChicken she had dealt with. She did something that threw me off-kilter in the best way possible. She lovingly and calmly asked us to unpack my anger together.

Spicy was caught off guard, because no one had ever asked her to unpack her anger. Not even therapists she had seen when she was younger. Spicy was just labeled an "angry teenager" or "hormonal" or "bipolar" by everyone around her. She was dismissed as such when growing up, so this was completely new to me. As a result of this woman's lack of resistance to Spicy, there was nothing to resist. To my epic surprise, Spicy was curious and engaged and, for the first time in her entire life, she was game to talk it out.

As Spicy was explaining to the woman what had happened, the woman calmly listened. She absorbed it all without taking a single ounce of it personally. This divine and majestic woman was a master at taming the Spicy within.

And, hello, I had just met her, so of course it wasn't personal. It was all my own anger issues rising up, and she was just another object for my angry outbursts. But she did the absolutely counter-instinctual and yet totally intuitive thing that day. She listened instead of engaging with or defending herself against Spicy.

After the woman listened to Spicy and asked questions to better understand what I had experienced in the hour plus that led up to her arrival, she finally responded. She said, "So it sounds like you made a subconscious decision that no matter what happened you were going to *choose* to be angry? Am I hearing that correctly?"

Insert that big-eyed emoji of shock.

My mind began bending as I began to digest and understand the truth bomb that had just been dropped on me. Holy shitballs, yes. The only way that I was going to be "happy" was if she was legitimately, exactly and precisely on time. However, even if she had been on time, I am sure Spicy would have gotten super creative and found something else to be mad about.

Later, I asked myself where else this pattern was showing up in my life. Oh, you know, only *everywhere*.

This was the moment I also got real and took a look at how rampant energies of perfection were getting tangled up in my life. If I was projecting that expectation of perfection outward toward others, who else do you think I might have been treating that way? Who else was I demanding perfection from if they didn't want to be on the receiving end of Spicy's rage?

Oh, that's right—*me*. I have learned that when Spicy starts coming out to play it is a clue that I am actually in massive need of some majorly epic Me Time.

So to all of my fellow Spicys out there: Please hear this. Spicy is *not* protecting and safeguarding your power. Spicy is handing it away like a hot potato. Please, for the love of unicorns and sparkles and all that is magic in this universe, when you are in Spicy mode, do yourself *and* the world a favor. Pause. Stop. Don't move.

Time to chill!!!

Being in public will make it worse! You are angry, and that is yours and yours alone to explore. If it is anyone else's fault or you believe the fault lies anywhere other than inside of you, you are handing your power away. If you lose your shit on someone and then you justify that it is somehow their fault, you are handing your power away. If you can't stop thinking about an injustice and somehow it is someone else's fault for you having wasted all of this time and energy, please realize that you are handing your power away.

Remember: how you feel, think, act, and believe are all yours. What you choose to do and not do with the stories you make up in your head, that is all you boo. Whether or not someone honors your boundaries of time and energy and what is ok with you and what is not ok, all yours too.

Spicy is an inside job. Go inside. Get curious about what is really going on. Take your power back.

Power Play

You know the drill. Get your pen and journal out and let's explore. What are some things you notice that make you angry on a recurring basis? Traffic? Bad drivers? Something someone you love does that drives you crazy? Take inventory. Write it all down.

Now, take each one and explore deeper:

✦ What are you *actually* **upset about**? I mean, you can't seriously be handing your power away to traffic, can you? You're going to let something that is inevitable just ruin your day, just like that? Come on, you are more powerful than that!

✦ How are you an **active participant** in the anger? *Hint, hint:* How are you expecting something to be different than it actually is? When you find yourself doing this, shift to allowing it to be how it *actually* is and solution-storm from there.

So, if you are expecting someone to be different from who they are, try allowing them to be exactly as they are. Try to explore ways you could shift how you relate to them as they are, not as you wish they'd be. If you are expecting there to be no traffic when there clearly is traffic, ask yourself:

How might I spend my time in traffic in ways that I could actually enjoy myself?

Stop expecting someone else to change and start focusing on yourself. Consider these questions:

✦ **If you were to take your power back** and own your part, what might YOU do differently that would help you shift the pattern?

✦ **If you really want to do some deep soul work** with Spicy ask, "What's the sadness underneath the anger?"

I shit you not, the minute you shift into feeling the feels that the anger is masking, you will set yourself free. Counter-instinctual, yet totally intuitive.

✓ *What are you sad about?*

✓ *What do you wish was different?*

✓ *What is the pain underneath the anger?*

✓ *What is the true desire underneath the anger?*

Remember, when there are two Spicys relating with one another, no one is working on the solution. You'll just keep going round and round in crazy-making, explosive, toxic, soul-damaging circles until one of you finally decides to stop. One of you needs to focus on shifting out of Spicy in order to break the pattern and try something new. A new Who.

And guess which one of you you can control to make the shift? Yep. You, and only you. Stop trying to control the other person and change them and instead focus on these questions:

✓ *What do I want?*

✓ *Which Who would be the best version to move me in the direction I actually desire to go?*

Unless, of course, you enjoy those circles. In that case, just keep doing what you're doing boo.

AVATAR PROFILE

The Contortionist
(Side Hustle of Sister Mary Martyr)

What do I need to do more of, give more of,
or be more of to be liked and/or loved by you?

This version of you learned somewhere along the way that you having power is not on the menu of life and that you should bend and contort to others as if you are a contortionist performing in the circus. When you are experiencing the Contortionist, your significance is in giving, often overgiving at the expense of yourself. You may convince yourself you are noble and loving and generous. Yet, what you are really doing is people pleasing and avoiding your own soul work of learning how to draw clear boundaries.

The Contortionist is all about what is in service to others and not actually having any focus on self. You're *giving giving giving* and often with no boundary line for where the giving stops. You are subconsciously playing the martyr role without even realizing it, and you are doing it all in the name of love. When you are a Contortionist, you take on the role of a martyr, literally sacrificing yourself due to the belief that "giving is love."

Lots of self-sacrifice when you are in this Avatar! This can lead to overgiving, depletion, and burn-out. Before long, you have nothing left for you to give yourself. Often you find yourself subconsciously deflecting and refusing to receive when you are experiencing the Contortionist, because all of your energy is in the giving and you don't even have your receiving portal open!

When you are being the Contortionist, you will find that you are the one doing all of the work in relationships. You overfunction like your life depends on it and then are genuinely confused about how you keep manifesting "takers." Um, hello. Perpetual givers attract perpetual takers.

If you want to attract people into your life who are more balanced in both giving and receiving, then you get to take your power back and focus on investing your energies in becoming more balanced yourself. It's time for you to practice receiving to balance out that giving. Practice opening yourself up to receiving by asking for what you want. Speak up for yourself.

When you are experiencing the Contortionist, you will also notice that you dream of the days when magically and suddenly the takers will see all that you have given and finally acknowledge, appreciate, and celebrate you. In actuality, those are the very things you need to learn to give to yourself—acknowledgement, appreciation, validation, and celebration. You fantasize that they will get on board the giving train and convince yourself that that is when you will finally get to receive. Yet, in order to break this pattern and step back in your power, it is imperative that you start to address the reality.

The truth is, this person is a taker, as you've conditioned them to be. They take from you because you are by being a bottomless pit of giving. Unless you change, there will be no change. Yas. Truth. Focus on what you can change, which, of course, is you. You can only change you. That's where your true power is.

When you are experiencing yourself being the Contortionist you may find yourself asking, *What do they want? What do they need? How can I help them?* You will spend your time consumed, thinking about all the ways you could help solve everyone else's problems, often times masterfully putting off your own.

News flash! Your problems are your Power Source, and other people's problems are their Power Source. So, you are actually getting power completely contorted in this Avatar, because you are stealing other's power while avoiding your own and calling it "giving," "love," and being "helpful."

Power Play

To take your power back when you find yourself in the Contortionist or Sister Mary Martyr Avatar, practice focusing on your own needs. You can do this by asking yourself the following questions. Make sure to get that journal and pen out right now if this is an avatar that needs some of your love and attention. It's time to clean things up in order to uplevel to a higher vibration. Let's rock!

- ✦ What do you **want**?

- ✦ What do you **need**?

- ✦ What support do you want and need **in this moment**?

- ✦ How might you **give these things to yourself**?

- ✦ Who might you ask to **support you** in this moment?

Practice Receiving

What might it look like to receive in your day to day life? Examples to get you started might include saying thank you when someone gives you a compliment, accepting help when someone offers it even if it is something you can do for yourself, or accepting someone's offer to treat you to something. Look at the world around you and all the ways it is trying to give you abundance.

How might you be accidentally saying no to abundance because you are so committed to giving that you are subconsciously renouncing and not receiving? With expanded consciousness comes new choice. Now that you are aware of where you are blocking yourself, you can consciously choose to show up as a new you next time and practice receiving.

Find sacred spaces where you get to be the receiver and not the giver. For example, you may get a massage and give yourself full permission to really receive the body work and relaxation. Perhaps you may choose to work with a therapist or life coach where they hold sacred space for you to receive the attention being all on you and your soul growth, so that you can continually move forward and expand and grow. (If you are looking for an intuitive life coach, hit me up, I am your girl!)

Or maybe you attend Meetup Groups, adventure communities, or classes on something you'd love to learn more about. Consider joining personal development events or communities where everything is already planned out for you. All you have to do is just show up, practice being present, and receive.

Resist the urge to give or people please in the conscious receiving spaces you create for yourself. Be mindful and present to the fact that this is your sacred space to receive. Let each opportunity be an experiment to grow in your receiving abilities. When your old urges to *give give give* come up, practice anchoring back in your intention to receive.

When you find yourself in the Contortionist, it's a good reminder that you are out of balance. It is time to get back to you. It is time to focus on what you want and need and to give to yourself. Ask for the support that you want and need, then ask yourself, *How can I create even more balance in my day today?*

Explore these questions:

- ✓ *We cannot create something if we do not know what we are creating. So give yourself permission to explore the possibilities. What might a balanced relationship look like?*

- ✓ *If you were showing up more balanced, how might that look? What might you stop doing? What might you start doing instead?*

Consider the love, appreciation, the celebration, and the acknowledgment you are hoping to receive from the outside world, and find ways you can give that to yourself every day. It is not uncommon for you, when you are tapping into the Contortionist Avatar, to give all of your love away and not save any for you.

- ✓ *What if you got to give all that amazing love to yourself?*

- ✓ *What might that look like?*

In moments when you feel an addictive pull to give to others, stop and give that love to yourself. This isn't about not giving to others. Trust me, you are great at giving, so you will never stop being loving and kind to others. There is no need to worry about that. This is about learning to give to yourself.

All the relationships you will experience in life are a direct result of Who you are showing up as. So, when you find yourself contorting to the world around you and overgiving, in hopes that somewhere along the way you will get your own needs met from others, remember that what you are craving from the world around you is often the very thing you need to stop and give to yourself.

AVATAR PROFILE

The Helper

I will do my absolute best to read your mind and anticipate your every need!!

The source of significance for The Helper is in being perceived as being "helpful." When you are operating from the Helper role, you may give information that no one has asked you for and offer insights, opinions, and advice—again, that no one actually asked you to provide. Usually the insights that you are offering aren't even something you have done yourself but rather something you learned about in a book, from a podcast, or on TV. You might be prone to pass on an article.

If by chance you have actually been through a similar thing yourself, this version of you feels that there is only one way through and it's your way. Thank God the Helper was there to share the one and only way with them before it was too late!

God forbid anyone asks The Helper to stop "helping" them. The Helper is crushed when this happens. They may act as if somehow someone wanting to do something on her own is a reflection of The Helper not being loved, cherished, and appreciated. This Avatar has a difficult time with boundaries and often feels attacked when others are not interested in the help being offered.

In experiencing this version of you, you may find yourself walking through life looking for ways to be "helpful" and constantly jumping in to offer assistance—even with complete strangers. The Helper often spends more time and energy scanning what is going on at other people's tables than being fully present with the people at their own table. If you see an injustice, The Helper will jump in. Thank God The Helper was there! What would anyone have done without the Helper?!

For The Helper, the validation of love and worth comes from the outside world. The Helper's worth relies solely on other people allowing you to take what belongs to them—their soulwork—and doing the work for them, enabling the shit out of them and stealing their power all in the name of being helpful.

Power Play

Practice being present in your own life. Instead of scanning a room and or trying to see how you can help the people around you, just relax. Breathe. Enjoy the moment. Trust that if someone actually needs something, that person will tell you. That is their power to own.

Give yourself permission to let go of the mind-reader attempts to desperately try to anticipate another person's needs. Take that helpfulness and help yo-self. You can do this by asking yourself the following questions. Make sure to get that journal and pen out right now if this is an avatar that needs some of your love and attention to clean up in order to uplevel to a higher vibration. Let's rock!

✦ **How do you feel?** What are the feelings of your own that you are accidentally overlooking while paying such close attention to how everyone else feels and and what they want and need?

✦ What do you **want**?

✦ What do you **need**?

✦ What would **excite and delight** you? What would allow you to experience even more joy in this moment?

Practice honoring yourself and being fully present for you. What a gift you can be to others when they get to experience you being fully present, relaxed, and at ease. The amount of love and connection that you will get to experience as a result will blow your damn mind. Relax. Breathe. Take the cape off and enjoy the moment.

✓ *What is it in your own life that you could focus on to move you forward?*

✓ *What areas of growth for your own self-development could use some of that helpful attention you so freely give to others?*

Playfully let people know that you are giving up your attempts at being a mind-reader. Suggest to them that, if they need anything at all, all they have to do is ask. Tell them that you trust that in the future they will let you know what they need and hand back their power.

If your particular breed of The Helper is super super busy reading other people's minds, it may be because you subconsciously think that that is how it works. You may even believe that others should be reading your mind too. If this is the case, practice asking for what you want.

Practice voicing your needs. Use your words.

✓ *What do you want help with?*

✓ *What kind of support do you need?*

Ask for it out loud, clearly and directly, and be open to receive it. You may also wish to explore ways to create an even more powerful source of love and connection with others. Get curious. Consider the following questions to create new opportunities for connection and a better experience in relationship.

◆ If you were to connect in new ways that do not include you feeling responsible to help them, what are some **ways that you might connect** with them?

◆ If, for example, you were to focus instead on things you both have in common—**common interests**, common likes, common activities, common goals, and common desires, what might that look like?

✦ What might it be like to create connection by **cultivating experiences** that are based in common interests and desires and bring all participants joy?

You will notice that you not only get higher vibration points of connection and relationships, you will also have a ton more energy when you are no longer attempting to read everyone else's mind. You don't have to hustle for love and worthiness by being helpful all the time. In fact, that low vibration energy of caring too much what others think about you is often the very thing getting in your way of true love and connection and depths of intimacy.

TAKE YOUR POWER BACK!

You are worthy and so damn lovable exactly as you are. Give yourself permission to act accordingly and just be.

#powerfulAF

AVATAR PROFILE
The Fixer
(Mr. or Mrs. Fix-It)

Everything is broken, and I can fix it all.
At your service!

The Fixer does *all* the heavy lifting. This Avatar believes that others are broken and that she, The Fixer, is the only one who can truly fix them and or solve whatever their problems are. This Avatar is doing *all* the work for others, not to mention stealing other's power and enabling them not to do a damn thing for themselves.

When experiencing this Avatar you may hear yourself say, "But they need me," followed by a whole ton of reasons the person is powerless and so you *have* to do it for them. How convenient that you, as the Fixer, have so many reasons to steal the other person's power and avoid your own soul growth, eh?

When The Fixer is showing up in your life you will find yourself drowning in an endless sea of "broken" and "powerless" souls. So many people to rescue and so little time in a day! You are utterly exhausted, depleted, and drained, but it was all worth it because you "saved" people.

Without you, where would they be? I mean, maybe they'd have a chance to learn to swim for themselves if you stopped being a human life raft every time they jump in a pool to learn?

Maybe? Just sayin'. Wink, wink.

When you experience yourself as The Fixer, you will attract people into your life and inner circle who are "projects," and you'll be left to wonder why you keep attracting such dysfunction. The Fixer will inform you, of course, that it is because you are "gifted" and this is the soul work you were put here on this planet to do. After all, if you didn't step in and help, you would be wasting your gifts. Oy vey! Oh, the justifications you make for stealing power!

The Fixer may be investing a lot of time speaking up for others and standing up on their behalf. The Fixer calls this courageous and noble, but the truth is that you are actually just sending a message to the people that you are speaking for that you think they are too weak to speak for themselves. Truth bomb yo.

Many times, you are not actually taking yourself and your own needs into consideration at all. You're too busy fixing others and there never seems to be enough time left over to work on your own stuff. Again, how convenient to get to avoid your own soul work, eh? You hide in the courage you give to others, yet the one who could benefit most from your courage and help is *you*.

Power Play

Focus on yo' damn self. Hahaha. I say that so lovingly. Seriously though, take all that courage and use it for *you*. Stop stealing power from others. Instead, be a beacon of light for what is possible when you are courageous for your own damn self. What better way to help them learn to do it for themselves too?

Let others learn to speak up for themselves as they watch you guide the way through embodied action. See how they get it by you speaking up for you, instead of you taking their power and speaking up for them. Imagine how powerful they will feel when they learn how to speak up for themselves.

Be the leader of light through embodied action. You can do this by asking yourself the following questions. Make sure to get that journal and pen out right now if this is an avatar that needs some of your love and attention to clean up in order to uplevel to a higher vibration. Let's rock!

✦ What are the **problems** that belong to you and your own soul work that you are too busy avoiding while fixing everyone else?

✦ What is it about yourself that you **feel is broken**? You cannot believe something about others that you do not also already think about yourself on some level. Boom. Truth bomb. Check yo' projections.

✦ What if they **actually don't need you?** What disempowering stories does your subconscious mind make up about what that might mean about you as a person? How true are those disempowering stories, actually? What might be more empowering beliefs and stories instead? How might you show up if you believed those new empowering beliefs and stories?

✦ **What are your own dreams** that you are putting off until tomorrow? What might life look like if you were to give yourself permission to start giving your own dreams just as much energy and attention as you give to the problems and solutions others have?

✦ What is the **worst thing** that might happen if you gave up being responsible for everyone else's problems and solutions?

✦ **What is the best thing** that might happen if you gave up being responsible for everyone else's problems and solutions?

✦ **If you truly believed** that all beings were incredibly powerful, how might you show up differently with the people you previously looked at as "broken" and "powerless"?

✦ **If you believed you were truly powerful** how might you show up in your own life, in your own soul growth and dreams, and in a new and even more empowering way for yourself and the world?

When you find yourself in The Fixer, gift yourself the courage to go within. Focus on your own soul growth, and boldly move in the direction of your dreams. Lead the path of change by *being* the change you wish to gift to the world.

Leverage Your Low Vibe Avatars

We covered some of the most common low vibe Avatars that hand your power away, avoid power all together, or steal other people's power and call it love. There are other Avatars that are pretty standard equipped, stock model, package offerings that we all experience at some point, such as: Comfy Slob, Procrastinista / Procrastinisto, Ruley McRulerson (oh, so many rules), Perfectionista / Perfectionisto, Saboteuress / Saboteuro, and The Fantasizer.

In addition, everyone has an Inner Child Avatar. Most of us have many versions of us that got frozen in times of misunderstandings, misinterpretations, and or traumas that we experienced in our earlier years. While we come into this world with purity of power, we are often frozen in trigger points and wounds that wreak havoc throughout our lives, often without us even knowing it consciously. So, as you give yourself permission to explore any and all Avatars that may be getting in the way of the very things that you want most, make sure to give some extra love attention and care to whichever versions of you represent your Inner Child Whos.

Pay attention to your low vibe Avatars, especially the ones we have covered in depth, as they will rule you and literally steal life from your years if you let them. When it comes to dealing with Avatars, consciousness and awareness are your superpowers. If you want to dig deeper in Avatar play, head over to the website and check out the Avatar programs that are available or connect with me for one-on-one work. Be sure to leave your email at the bottom of the website so that you can be in the know as new thangs launch www.epicsexyyou.com.

Now that you've got a feel for Avatar descriptions, if there are any other lower vibration versions of you getting in the way, identify them. Name them something playful that will make you laugh and get to know each one better. Paint a crystal clear identity of who they are, what they look like, what they typically wear, how they feel in your body, the stories that drive them, and their primary intentions as they navigate life.

Get to know your low vibe Avatars so that you can be more aware of them when they show up and take center stage. If you remain super conscious when a low vibe Avatar is present, that Avatar can't wreak too much havoc in your life. Any time you find yourself feeling any way other than how you desire to feel in life ask yourself, "Who is driving this human body suit?" Identify the Avatar or Avatars at play.

Once you know Who you are dealing with, you can play with the questions for those particular versions of you and take your power back. After you have assessed Who you are dealing with and you've taken your power back from that Avatar, you can then ask the following questions.

✦ What do I want to **experience**?

✦ Who will be an **even more powerful version** of me that is in alignment with my desire?

✦ How might the new version **show up** in a way that will help me move in the direction of growth and get me closer to where I am craving to go?

That, my friend, is where creating Power Avatars comes in! You do not have to live at the mercy of your motley crew of conditioned Avatars who are used to running the show. No, you can create your own Avatars—ones who are aligned with your deepest dreams and desires for your life.

Creating Powerful Avatars

As you learn to consciously create your Who, you will awaken to infinite possibilities. You will discover just what you are capable of and just how damn powerful you are.

The first step in being the Master Creator of your Who is to be super conscious and fully aware of Who is getting in your way, which is what we just went through. Now you can be on the lookout for those lower vibration Avatars and reel them back in before they take over and King Kong your entire Dreamtown.

The next step is to leverage your powerful Avatars and also consciously create new ones so you can give birth to new possibilities in your life—possibilities that you most certainly do not have access to when you are embodying a low vibe Avatar.

Current High Vibe, Powerful Avatars

First let's look at Who you have already created that is working *for* you. Consider these questions:

✦ What are the areas of life that you are **slaying**?

✦ What are the areas of life where you **feel most on fire**?

✦ Where do you feel you are an unshakable, **powerful version of yourself**? While working out? In a close relationship? As a parent? In your business or career? In a particular friendship? With your relationship with yourself?

Take a moment and identify several areas and relationships in your life where you tend to have consistent forward movement, experience loads of joy, and feel pretty excited to be you. Then, one by one, explore:

✦ What is the **primary desire** present in that area of your life?

✦ What are the **common paradigms, thought patterns, and beliefs** that drive how you handle and navigate the inevitable bumps of life in that particular area?

✦ What are some **questions** that tend to be on repeat inside your head when you are navigating that area of your life?

✦ **Consciously explore:** What are the primary sources of significance for you in this area of your life?

What is it that makes you feel important and allows you to have meaning in this area of your life and why? Is it the growth you experience? Is it the contribution you are making in the world or in another person's life? Is it the love and connection you experience? Is it the fact that there is a ton of variety and spontaneity?

Or perhaps there is a ton of stability and security that you get to experience? Perhaps it's that you have the freedom to do what you want, when you want and how you want to do it. Maybe this is an area of your life where you feel like you get to be you—the most unapologetic, unfiltered you who is appreciated and celebrated for being you.

✦ If you were to **name this version of you**, what name might you choose?

✦ If you were to give this Who a **theme song**, what might it be?

Get curious and explore. Get playfully curious about how your current low vibe Avatars and your current high vibe Avatars are different. This clarity will help you become even more conscious about Who is Who, and will help you determine which Who specifically is showing up for you in any given moment. It will help you spot each Avatar even faster and get ahead of those sneaky sneaky low vibers.

Where else might you consciously use the current high vibe Avatars in your life? What might be another area where they could excel? Get creative! Try different Whos on for size and see which Whos do what in each life area, relationship, and situation. Play with them. Feel them out. Ditch what isn't working and keep doing what serves you!

Create Your Own Power Players

OK, so now you know Who is getting in your way and Who is serving you in certain areas of your life. But there are so many more possibilities of Who you can be beyond the Whos you currently access. You will quickly realize that if you take a power player from one area of your life and try to put them into another area, it may not align so well.

Perhaps you have a Boss Avatar that slays at work, and then you accidentally bring that energy into a relationship. You may quickly realize that your partner is like, "Yo, I don't work for you boo. You better check that shit at the door."

So then what?

Which powerful Who are you consciously bringing once you cross the threshold from business into relationship? These are the kinds of powerful questions you get to ask yourself when you play with the art of Avatars, consciously creating your Who.

So, you may find yourself asking at some point:

✓ *Who can I consciously bring in to areas where I might be getting perpetually stuck?*

✓ *What if there is an area of life where I don't have a current Avatar that would be a good fit for what I want?*

This second scenario is most likely the true root of why you are stuck in the first place. Because you don't have access to a powerful Who yet, you have not found a clear path to success and all the goodness you want to create in your life. These instances afford you an opportunity to create a new Who!

WOOO! YAS! This is exciting, juicy, magical shit!

Power Play

Pick an area of your life where you would like to see some forward movement, create more joy, or experience something completely new for yourself. Get that journal and pen out and let's play with creating a new Who!

✦ What do you want to **create** in this area of your life?

✦ What specifically do you want to **experience**?

✦ How do you want to **feel**?

✦ And **what else** do you want? What else? What do you want? What do you really really want? And what else? Get all up in the desire. Paint a clear, vibrant picture of your desire.

Remember that true power is about desire, intention, and alignment. So once you have desire anchored in, it's all about creating a Who that is in alignment with that desire. This Avatar can consciously move you in the direction you want to go.

Create Your Who

✦ If there was a Who that was in alignment with your particular desires, what might be some of the **empowering paradigms**, thought patterns, and beliefs they would have?

✦ Consider this new Who that is **in alignment** with the desires you just mapped out. How might they navigate the inevitable bumps of life in ways that would still allow you to move steadily forward in the direction you want to go—no matter what you encounter along the way?

✦ If there was a Who that was in alignment with your particular desires, what might be some **questions** they would ask on repeat inside your head when navigating that area of your life to move you consciously in the direction of all of those desires?

✦ How might this version of you **approach growth** in a way that best serves you and your desires?

✦ How might this version of you **contribute to the world**, to yourself, and to others around you in ways that are in alignment with what you want?

✦ How might this version of you consciously create and allow space for **variety and/or spontaneity** in empowering ways that are in alignment with what you want?

✦ How might this version of you consciously create and allow space for **stability, security, and certainty** in alignment with what you want?

✦ How might this version of you consciously **honor your own freedom** to be unapologetically you, appreciated and celebrated for being you *and* completely in alignment with what you want?

✦ If there was a Who that was in alignment with your particular desires, how might they **show up physically** and invite you to dress for the part?

✦ If there was a Who that was in alignment with your particular desires, **how might they talk**?

✦ If there was a Who that was in alignment with your particular desires, **how might they walk**?

✦ What is a **name** for this Who? Pick a name that anchors in the essence of how you want to feel.

✦ Who would you **need to be** in order to get forward movement in that area of your life?

✦ Give this Who a **theme song**. What song will it be?

Now that you have a clearer picture, what is a goal that this version of you would be excited and delighted to work towards? Choose a goal that, in order for you to achieve that next level, you'd sure as shit have to stretch into a new you. Give your new Who something to strive for and move toward! A clear goal is the fuel that allows you to be pulled forward in life by your Whos, rather than you aimlessly drifting through life and allowing your low vibe Avatars who lack direction to bully you and others.

Now that you are armed with this new Who consciousness, you will have an infinite array of choice when you feel stuck in your life. Next time you feel stuck, ask yourself:

✦ Who is **currently operating** in this human body suit?

✦ What do I want and **which Who can help me** get what I want to experience?

✦ What are some **alternative options** of Whos that might be in even more powerful alignment for what I desire to experience in this moment?

✦ If I don't currently have access to a powerful Who to honor the intention and desires of the moment, then **Who might I create** that can come in and move my energy of desire forward?

Who you are at any given moment in time is part of your own creation. You have the power to explore the world and move through it in whatever way you would like to experience it. Consciously check in with yourself every step of the way and correct your course continuously to ensure that you are moving in a direction of expansion and growth that you truly desire.

Trust that everything in life is happening *for* you. Every moment in life is an opportunity to expand into new versions of you—versions that allow you to see just how infinitely expansive and powerful you truly are. You are so powerful. I cannot wait to see all of the Whos you have fun creating!

POWER SOURCE #2

POWER OF TRIBE

POWER QUOTE

*You are the average of the five people
that you spend the most time with.*
Jim Rohn

When your inner circle is not in alignment with where you want to go and who you want to be, it is like a fire hose of water aimed directly at the flames of your desire. However, when your inner circle *is* in alignment with where you want to go and who you want to be, it is like a pyromaniac pouring lighter fluid directly onto the fires of your momentum. Every new version of you that you step into will require a new elevated vibration of tribe.

Some of your current people will come with you as you expand and some will not. That is OK. It doesn't mean that you need to let them go entirely, it may just mean that you spend less time with those who are no longer in alignment with the current direction you are headed.

Misalignment Example

When I decided to quit drinking, what do you think happened in the world around me? Well, for starters, when the company I worked for at the time had happy hours or events that revolved around drinking and I chose not to go, I was told I was "not being a team player." I would explain that I had a drinking problem and

141

felt it was best to avoid social outings that involved alcohol. Still, I was deemed "not a team player" and was informed that my decision not to attend company events was hurting my reputation in the company.

When I did go to work events and people found out I was not drinking, they would reply with, "Don't judge me." I kid you not, they were not joking. They were serious as can be. They legitimately felt judged by my own personal decision to not drink. I had people say, "Well, look at you on your high horse."

The truth was that I could never stop after one drink, I constantly blacked out, and I absolutely did not love myself or my life when I drank. This is why I decided to get sober. Yet, somehow, now that I had made this decision for myself, I was deemed to be on a high horse? What?

Sobriety was the best decision for me. My decision had nothing to do with anyone else, but time and time again people projected their own self-judgments onto me as if I was somehow judging them. Really, they were judging themselves, not me.

When I quit drinking I was told by people I genuinely liked and cared for that, "There is no way you are going to keep this up." I was told I was "lame" and "boring." I had friends say to me, "You are more fun when you drink." If by "fun" you mean that I was the biggest ass in the group and entertained others while killing my liver, sabotaging any and all romantic relationships that came into my life, and giving my friends front row seats to the shitshow that was my life, then, yes, I was so much fun. WOO!

I had friends say, "You don't have a drinking problem. Come on, let's go out, and you can have just one." In a moment of my life where I felt so proud of a decision that I made, instead of being celebrated by my outside world I was being shamed, blatantly disregarded, judged, and discouraged.

This will happen to you as you grow. Just know that you are not crazy, and it is a normal process of expansion and upleveling. This is why it is so important to maintain consciousness with who is around you every step of your journey.

I began to realize I was surrounded by clients, coworkers, and friends whose primary sources of entertainment, socializing, and connection were drinking and going out to parties and bars. This made perfect sense, because that was my world for the 10-plus years prior to my decision to make the shift into sobriety. The truth was that the direction of my life had shifted, and I was no longer in alignment with who I was hanging around. I needed to do the work to shift who I was investing my time and energy with in order to create a more optimal alignment with my new desires.

I had to get real honest with myself. I had to choose *who I wanted to be* over who others wanted me to be. I had to let go of how others felt about me and focus on how I felt about me. I had to stop worrying so much about how others may be hurt if I made changes and focus on myself.

Alignment Example

On the flip side of subconscious misalignments in relationships is the power of consciously creating relationships that are in alignment for all parties. When you consciously create your inner circle or tribe, it can be like hacking into the energy circuits to give you the most forward-propelling jolts of all time.

During my most recent life upgrades, as I was stepping into an even more expansive and powerful version of myself, I got super crystal clear on who I wanted to become next and who I wanted to surround myself with. With that newfound clarity of desire and direction, I was able to consciously assess the alignment of desires and direction of each person I encountered. I leveraged that clarity and applied a conscious selection process that helped me determine who I chose to invest my time and energy with.

I had the most fortunate opportunity to meet someone who was also an entrepreneur, who was always up for trying new things, who was courageous and danced with her fear. She was up for the continual challenge of stepping more and more outside of her comfort zone. She mirrored back to me when I was getting in my own way and playfully received the same in return. She continuously inspired me to dream even bigger every step of the way. It is rare to find someone who can keep up with the pace that I stretch and grow. Yet every step of the way there she was, and many times she was leading the pace.

Every time I was with her, I was able to assess how I felt. Each time I felt more energized and more inspired to become an even more powerful version of myself. So I would consciously choose to spend more time with her. Eventually, after enough points of connection and getting to know her over a period of time, an incredibly beautiful, conscious, powerful, and magical inner circle tribe alignment was birthed.

As a result of our alignment in our desires to grow our businesses and blow our own damn minds, I found the courage within to apply for and do a TEDx Talk titled "Power is an Inside Job." I wrote a second book. Designed and launched an Epic AF (as f*ck) tank top collection for the tribe. Did an Audiobook to accompany the first book *Epic Sexy You*. And rolled out six new programs for my tribe.

Meanwhile she achieved a six-figure stretch goal in six weeks and more than doubled her business income over the course of the entire year. She faced a lifelong fear of heights and climbed to the top of an indoor climbing wall. Together we learned how to fly a plane, flew in an outdoor wind tunnel, did trapeze, conquered an up-in-the-air ropes course, and swam with sharks. Her motto was "F*ck the Comfort Zone" and damn did we ever step into courage portal after courage portal and face our fears.

On top of all that awesomeness we had a shit ton of fun doing it all! We set big goals and celebrated every epic feat with some massively motivating rewards. We went to Disney three times in a six-month period. We took flight lessons. We went hang gliding. We learned Bachata. We met lemurs, sloths, seals, sting rays, penguins, dolphins, and kangaroos. We went snorkeling. We took golf lessons. I could go on and on and on, but you get the point, eh? Alignment brings juicy mind blowing magic!

This epic inner circle tribe magic didn't happen haphazardly, although there was plenty of serendipitous synchronicity that was at play. The co-creation of our powerful momentum was conscious and wildly aligned. You can do the same for yourself.

Finally, remember that alignment is fluid, not static. You are constantly writing new chapters in your life. Sometimes someone is wildly aligned in one chapter and no longer aligned with the new chapters you write. The roles they play may shift, evolve, and change over time. They may even depart in your next chapter.

That is all OK. It is all normal. It does not take away from the magical and powerful alignment that they offered in the chapters where they truly shined. That being said, give yourself permission to check in with each new version of you that emerges along your journey of expansion, and feel your way through the alignment of each person in your inner tribe every step of the way.

Align consciously, align accordingly.

You as Creator Self

The true essence and intention of leveraging tribe as a power source is for you to consciously embrace that you are the creator of your own world. You get to decide Who you show up as and who you invest your time and energy into.

Make sure you do so consciously.

Create alignment intentionally and purposely versus falling into the power trap of you being at the effect of the world and the relationships around you. Beware of the power trap of excuses that may come up around family and longtime friends. You may discover that you are no longer in alignment with some of the people in your life, yet the majority of your time and energy goes to them and you continuously feel as if you do not have a choice. You are so much more powerful than that. Own your power of choice.

Finally, be aware of the power trap of feeling as if other's resistance being projected onto you is somehow yours. It is not. Their resistance to your growth is simply an indicator that they would prefer that you stay status quo alongside them so that they don't have to face their own exponential possibilities and potential for growth.

Let me repeat that. Their resistance to change has nothing to do with you. Just remember that in the midst of the crazy-making you may find yourself in when those in your inner circle get weird about you growing! Sometimes, in the moments that you expect the most celebration from your loved ones, you will actually encounter the most resistance. While people are busy dealing with their own resistance, you can get busy consciously crafting intentional relationships with people who are willing to walk alongside you and add fuel to your dreams.

Power Play #1

Before you can explore your own optimal alignment possibilities, you have to know what you want. That consciousness of desire will inform you about Who you need to show up as to be in alignment with what you want. It will give you a framework for how you decide who to invest your time and energy in.

So take out a pen and your journal. Let's get at it!

+ What do you **want most** in life?

+ What **direction** do you want to go in?

+ What does **life look like** where you are headed?

+ Who are you **becoming**?

+ Who do you **want to become**?

+ What do you want to **become more** of?

+ What do you want to **experience more of**?

+ How do you **want to feel** when you are with others?

- How do you **want others to feel** when they are with you?

- What are your **standards** in life, both for yourself and for those you allow to be in close proximity?

Let me give you some of my own personal examples to help ignite some of your own ideas:

- I want to live **an Epic and Legendary Life**. I want to surround myself with others who want the same for themselves. I want to be around people who are willing to go through and grow through the discomfort of leaving their warm and fuzzy comfort zone.

- I want to **surround myself with** those who are willing to stretch into new levels where they will create new versions of themselves and who want to share that journey of expansion.

- I want to surround myself with **people who love life**!

- I want to surround myself with **people who love who they are** and who love what they do.

- I want to **be inspired** and to inspire.

- I want to **play and have fun,** laugh, co-create adventure experiences, and make epic memories together!

✦ I want to feel like my **peeps have my back**, and I want them to feel like I've got theirs.

✦ I want to feel like my peeps are **adding value** and light and love to my life and that I add value and light and love to theirs. We make each other's lives easier and much more fun and full.

✦ I want to experience a profound **depth of connection** and authenticity.

✦ I want to have **open lines of communication** that allow for radical honesty with love.

✦ I want to be **a mirror** to my peeps' blind spots and to have them be a mirror for me too. I would like to make sure that there is an upfront agreement to say it, to mirror it back, to point it out. To me, that is true strength in tribe. I know there are a ton of places where I have blind spots. To have a tribe surrounding me to mirror back those blind spots, to playfully tease me when I'm getting in my own way, and to challenge the BS and limiting beliefs that are getting in my way— holy powerful tribe and inner circle of epic proportions!

✦ I want to **laugh**. I want to feel seen and heard, loved and appreciated for who I am. I want to surround myself with others that I feel the same about.

✦ I want to be surrounded by **courageous people** who not only follow their dreams, but who are also open to me supporting them on their path. I want them to encourage and support me in chasing my most epic and legendary self and life.

✦ I want to know they **celebrate** me as I celebrate them. I want to see them face their fears and try, try, try again in the pursuit of their deepest desires. Perfection is not required. Putting in the work is.

Now that I have shared some examples of my own, make sure to take some time and write out your own wants, desires, and standards. If you are at the point in your journey where you "don't know" what you want yet, perhaps start with what you don't want.

You know what feels shitty and what you'd like less of, so flip it. If it feels shitty to be surrounded by takers, then flip that to wanting more generous givers and a two-way street for the relationships in your life, where there is a beautiful and balanced exchange of give and take.

Think about who you are becoming. What might that person be like? What might feeling even better, even more empowered and joyous, look like? There is no right or wrong. There is only a spectrum of desire, and every day that you practice connecting to that desire that muscle will get stronger and stronger.

Just keep exploring! And what else might you want? And what else? And what else might feel good to experience in a close relationship? And what else? And who else might you like to show up as in life in a way that would allow you to be even more proud to be you? How could you feel even better and better every day?

Remember that growth is a journey. One step at a time boo. You've got this!

Once you've got some ideas on your wants, desires, and standards, explore further with these questions:

+ How might you **use these new standards** consciously every day as a selection criteria for who you invest your time and energy with and relate to?

+ How can you **live in greater alignment** with your desires?

+ **Who do you need to be** in order to do your part in showing up in a way that is in alignment with the type of relationship you crave to experience? Explore this for each and every relationship in your life.

As you are exploring your desires and standards, let me remind you that when you start to dream big you may trigger those around you who have yet to awaken to their own expansiveness. Some people may even tell you your standards are "too high" or that you're being "unrealistic." As Will Smith said, "Being realistic is the most common path to mediocrity." Give yourself permission to want what you want. Set your dream bar high and allow it to be an invitation for others to do the same.

POWER QUOTE

You will be too much for some people.
Those are not your people.
Unknown

Power Play #2

Now that you have identified what you want, where you would like to go, and Who you would like to be, let's assess your current inner circle. We are looking to bring any and all alignment and misalignment possibilities into your consciousness. Be on the lookout for what is serving you, so you can do more of that. Become aware of what is not serving you, so you can do less of that.

✦ Who do you **spend the most amount of time with** in any given day, week, month, or year? Think friends, family, coworkers, partners, etc.

✦ What is the amount of **time and energy you invest** with each person? Consider not only face-to-face time, but also virtual time, from phone conversations to email or instant messaging, from texts to social media. Who you are giving your thoughts and energy to?

✦ With each of the people you spend time with, look at **where they are in alignment** with your desires and standards, as well as with the direction you want to go, and where they are out of alignment. Get conscious. Do a deep dive for each person.

✦ Who are the people you **feel empowered by** when you are in their presence? Get curious about what factors are at play here.

✓ *How are you showing up differently with the people you feel empowered by as opposed to how you show up with people you feel disempowered by?*

✓ *How might you consciously bring even more of your expansive, powerful self with you everywhere you go?*

✓ *How might you structure your life to consciously spend even more time with people who you truly love?*

✓ *What are all of the ways that you love being you when you are with them?*

✦ Who are the people that leave you **feeling drained** when you are with them or after a visit? Get curious.

✓ *What are the factors that may be contributing to the drain?*

✓ *How are you being an active participant?*

✓ *How might you show up in a different way next time in order to experience less drain and stay even more in your power?*

Perhaps you could change the way you are showing up with them. Maybe you could decrease the frequency of your visits or shorten the amount of time and energy you are investing in them.

✦ Who are the people you spend time with and you **feel like you shrink** when you are around them?

    ✓ *How are you being an active participant in that shrinking pattern?*

    ✓ *What might you be able to do that allows you to show up differently with them next time?*

Again, focus on what you can control—*you!* Explore what it might look like for you to stay in your fullest expression of power the next time you are with them.

✦ Who may you need to **spend less time with** or even part ways from altogether in order for you to make more room for those who are in even more alignment?

✦ Who might you love to **carve out even more time** to consciously connect with?

Get honest with yourself about whether or not people are in alignment with who you are now and with who you want to become. Consider whether perhaps you have been settling for mediocrity. If you catch yourself justifying and rationalizing why "it's fine" or "it's ok" to spend a lot of time with people who are not in alignment with you and your goals, remember: settling is for suckers, you are not a sucker.

You are a powerful being who deserves so much more than a "good" life. You are so worth it. Give yourself the gift of consciously creating more alignment by choosing Who you show up as and with whom you are choosing to invest your time and energy. You are so powerful.

Remember that you have a choice in everything that you do. Take your power back and consciously create your life.

Power Play #3

Now that you have some new insights about the people in your current inner circle, let's play with all the ways that you might be able to consciously leverage desire to create even more of what you want to experience. This is your opportunity to declare Who you want to be in each of your relationships in life instead of feeling as if the relationships are happening to you.

Take your power back and become the Master Creator of your relationships and Who you show up as in each one. When focusing on change, remember that the only thing that you truly have the power to change is you.

It all starts with you. You are your greatest Power Source.

Leveraging Current Peeps

Give yourself the gift of upgrading the quality of your own inner circle, starting with the people that you already know and love.

◆ What, specifically, would you like to **invite your current peeps** into?

◆ What do you **want to experience more of** in each relationship? Do this for each relationship in your life.

◆ And how might you be able to be an active participant in the **creation of more** of that in your relationship?

◆ How might you invite those in your inner circle to **share this journey** of expansion with you? For example, who in your life needs to read this book? Who might you gift a copy of this book to so that they can be on the same page as you as you step into more and more heights of consciousness, magic, and true inner power?

TAKE YOUR POWER BACK!

You are the conscious creator of every single relationship in your life. If there are any relationships in your life where you are experiencing less than what you desire and you desire to keep these people in your life, then it is time to explore your part of the dance.

#powerfulAF

Remember, when you are a part of the problem you can be a part of the solution. How are you an active participant in the current less than desirable patterns you are experiencing in this relationship? What is it that you would like to experience instead? Accepting the person as they are, not as you wish them to be, how might you be an active participant in the creation of what you desire to experience with this person?

Finding New Peeps

You can also give yourself the gift of consciously creating and cultivating new relationships that are in alignment with the life you crave to live. Ask yourself:

+ What **types of people** would you love to spend more time with?

+ **Where** might these people be? Think outside the box. Even in a book, for example, you can dance with the author's energy, just like you are doing with me now. Think about virtual groups and online communities. It's amazing to watch the epic alignment of high vibration and cosmic expansion that happens when I host virtual group coaching programs, live immersion weekends, and events or retreats.

+ **Consider opportunities** for face-to-face meetings. Where might your people be? Where might they hang out?

✦ What **communities** might you join or social media feeds might you follow that will allow you to feel more of how you want to feel? Which ones may you need to unfollow in order to give yourself permission to be in even more authentic alignment with who you want to be and the direction you want to go in life?

If you can't find a community that lights you up, how might you be able to create it yourself? Explore what kind of community you really want to create and then leverage the resources available to you to broadcast an invitation to that kind of community. Perhaps you can leverage online resources, such as Meetup.com, where you can post your group idea. Perhaps you could put up flyers in your community where your kind of peeps may be looking.

You are the Master Creator of who you spend your time with, and sometimes that means having to be persistent and keep trying new and creative ways to make new connections until you make it happen. If you spend time with people who are not in alignment, you may be subconsciously settling. Get curious as to why you may be making the exceptions, and get radically honest with yourself as to what soul work of your own you may be avoiding by accepting mediocrity.

If you want an epic and legendary life, it is your responsibility to be conscious of who you allow into your physical and energetic real estate. Consciously create a powerful inner circle and tribe that is in alignment with your desired direction, all the while creating a Who that you love being. When you do this, your life will dramatically shift into mind-blowing trajectories of limitless expansion.

POWER SOURCE #3

DESIRE, COMMITMENT, AND ALIGNMENT

POWER QUOTE

Weak desire brings weak results, just as a small fire makes a small amount of heat.
Napoleon Hill

You get to have whatever the hell you want in life, and it starts with knowing what you want. Are you seeing a pattern here? This intentionally recurring question throughout our journey together is your critical first step:

What do you want?

To turn your desires into reality, you have to know what you want, you have to be truly committed to it, and you have to be in alignment with it. In this section we are going to talk about how to consciously leverage desire, commitment, and alignment to work for you so that you have a winning formula to create whatever it is that you want. Feel free to come back to this section over and over again with each new desire that emerges in your life.

Decide. Commit. Be All In.

Sometimes you think that you have made a decision about what you want, but you have not. You think that you are committed and say you are all in on that desire; yet, the truth is you are lying to yourself. It is a subconscious lie.

You may not even know you are doing it. You think you are completely on board with the dream. You believe that you are taking action toward that dream and the fulfillment of your desires. But the clue that you are not truly committed and all in comes when you really take a look at how you feel.

Are you feeling stuck? Are you feeling lethargic or resistant in any way? If so, it is time to play with increasing your level of desire and commitment.

Power Play

Grab yo' journal! Let's get at it!! Write out a whole list of desires that you would love to get traction on and see become a reality in your life. Then, pick your top three dreams or desires and do the following exploration. For each top desire explore:

✦ On a scale of 1 to 10, with 1 being not at all committed and 10 being fully committed, where would you rate your **current level of commitment** to each desire?

✦ How much **time, energy, thought, and action** are you giving to each desire?

This is where radical honesty with self comes in. You see, if you think you are at an 8, 9, or 10 on your commitment to your desire and yet you do not have what you desire and are not experiencing epic traction in that area, then you my friend are BYOB (Buying Your Own Bullshit).

Pay attention to the patterns that are emerging. Ask yourself:

+ How are you **interacting with** your desire?

+ Is there a possibility that you are **thinking you are committed** to action when really you are more committed to the idea of it?

+ On a scale of 1 to 10, 1 being 0% and 10 being 100% how would you rate **your desire level** for each of your top desires? How badly do you actually want each desire?

You may find, as I did, that the desire levels are in the ballpark of alignment with your commitment levels. If this is *not* the case and you found that you desire something at a 10 but are committed to it at a lower level, hold on. We will address that next up. First, let's look at what happens when you say you want something but have not rated that desire as high as you initially thought you would.

Low Desire Ratings

Pay attention as you read each potential block to feel what is most true for your top desires that have low desire ratings. Then, when we get to the Power Play, you can return to that block, ask yourself the relevant questions, and do the work.

When you uncover a low desire rating for something you actually do desire, here are a few blocks that may be getting in the way of the rating being higher:

+ **You may not think it is possible.** You may not be sure how to make it happen. Oh, that damn Ninja Mind addiction to How. If you find yourself in this boat, ask yourself, *What if it was possible? What might be some creative ways to make it happen?* Just sit with that possibility. *What else might you be able to try? And what else? And what else?*

Enlist your Possibilitarian friends to help you. Those are the friends that dream big, think outside the box, and swim in the endless wealth of possibility. Jam on some creative, out of the box ideas. And, please, for the love of unicorns, dreams, and abundance, do NOT ask your skeptical "Yeah, But" friends who have a problem and a "Yeah, But" for every solution.

Stay in the lane with your fellow dreamers. Or sit in the dream lane by yourself and immerse yourself in endless possibilities. *What else might you try? And what else? And what else? And what else?*

♦ **You may not be spending enough time on a daily basis investing in making that dream crystal clear and more and more juicy, yummy, and exciting.** Keep your focus on your dream so that you can really *feel it* every single day and remember why you want it. Play with questions that connect you to the feeling you will have when your dream is a reality. *What are all of the ways that your life will be different when the desire is a reality?*

Paint the picture. Make it crystal clear. Taste how yummy and juicy your life will be. Sit daily and write out your dream, meditate on it and envision it. Feel it in your body. Allow yourself to experience this feeling and you will start to feel pulled forward by the excitement you have for your desire.

- **You may be focusing your energy and attention on things that are easier.** My fall-back pattern is to focus on my business because I am good at it, and it feels good to be good at things. *Do I want an even more successful business?* Well, duh, yeah, of course I love growing my empire. It's so much fun.

    But the truth is that I will always be successful because of how much I love what I do. I love my clients and I love all the elements of running a business. I love being a life coach. I love getting to do event planning, writing, and everything else that I am so damn blessed to get to do. So, my growth in that arena of life is inevitable.

    However, someone who knows me well once said to me, "I feel like you could triple the empire that you've built. Yet, it will not bring you any more happiness unless you have someone to share your life with." Truth bomb. Amen. I want to share the journey with someone, co-creating life together, building together, and growing together. I want to have a partnership where we are supporting and celebrating one another. I see my partner and I dream chasing together, adventuring together, and building a home together, all the while committed to an epic and super conscious love.

    I can lie to myself and keep focusing solely on growing my business and buying my own BS that I'll shift my focus to epic love as soon as I wrap up whatever project I am working on at the moment. *Or I can admit that I am lying to myself and acknowledge that the truth is I will always have another project to get excited and delighted about. Further, I can acknowledge that it is going to take me deciding to commit fully and be all in on that desire if I want to turn my dreams into reality. That would also mean that I would have to get clear on painting the picture!*

What does epic love mean to me? What does life look like when I have it all? Epic love. Epic life. Epic empire. *What might my day-to-day life look like if I was committed to that desire, starting right now?* For starters, I'd probably leave my house more. You know, meeting actual human beings outside of my house and the grocery store. Yas. Truth bombs for all! Me too!

✦ **You may think that having what you want will actually cost you too much emotionally, mentally, physically, or financially.** You may think that what you want is competing with another desire, as if somehow you can only have one or the other. You may believe somehow if you have more success in your business you will have less time for fun. Or if you make time for an epic love that it will take away from your success. I challenge you to think about this:

What if you could have it all? What might that look like? Take the time to consciously create this new neural pathway that allows for what I call "The AND Factor." *What are all of the desires you want? And what else? And what else? And what else? And what might it look like if you got creative and made space for all of it in your epic and legendary life?*

You *can* have it all as long as you get creative and step into possibility. Remember, if you have never exercised your "have it all" muscle then it may be fatigued. You will need to keep practicing it in order to develop the muscle. Invest in you and your dreams. You are so worth it.

Practice practice practice.

Dream dream dream.

✦ **Desire levels are low sometimes because of the learning curve that you may foresee in your inevitable future.** Deep down, you know what will be required to turn that desire into reality. The good ol' Addiction to How may be taking center stage and wreaking havoc behind the scenes in your subconscious mind. "Yes, I want that," you say. "But how do I get it? I don't know! And I tried a couple of things and it felt hard and I don't get it, so I'll leave that for later. I need to learn more about it first."

This is the point at which you turn a blind eye to that desire and you BYOB (Buy Your Own Bullshit), when you give yourself all the reasons and justifications for focusing on others things "just for now." To walk yourself back into your desire gradually, you can ask yourself every single day:

✓ *What is one thing I can do to feed this desire today?*

✓ *What is one action I can take in 30 minutes or less today that will be an epic investment in my desire*

Lean in.

✦ **Desire levels may be low because it may not actually be your desire in the first place.** Ask yourself: Where did this desire come from? Whose desire was it? How did it creep into your desire space? And where else is that pattern of subconsciously taking on other people's desires showing up in your life?

✦ **You may even find through your deeper exploration of each desire that you don't actually even want what you thought you wanted**. If you bump into this, get curious. Ask: *When in your life was this desire an actual desire for you? When did this stop being a desire? What do you want now instead?* Remember, it is totally OK to change your mind and no longer want something you thought you once wanted. You are a powerful, evolving being. Allow your desires to evolve too.

Power Play

Get your journal and pen out, and get ready to explore and expand. Take time to go back through each of the Potential Blocks we just covered and explore which ones are the most common culprits that are getting in your way. Identify what it is specifically that you need to start doing and or stop doing in order to reclaim the forward movement that you crave to experience.

Low Commitment Levels

On the other hand, what if your desire level is high and you genuinely do want something, but your commitment level is low? When you find that you have a high desire level and a low commitment rating, it's time to ask yourself some new questions that allow you to go even deeper into *why* you want what you want.

Why do you want it? The why is your fuel. The compelling, juicy, yummy vision and anchored intention helps you re-engage with your passion and purpose every time you lose connection with what you are doing. Each time you consciously reconnect to your why, BOOM! In that moment, the commitment, excitement, and passion for your why comes right back.

Power Play

Let's explore your Why, shall we?! Get your journal and pen out, and get ready to explore and expand.

- ✦ **Why do you want it?** How will your life be different when you have honored your vision fully? What is *not* honoring your vision costing you? If 10 more years go by and you still have not honored that desire, then what does life look like? What does life feel like? What about when you are on your deathbed? What would it feel like to have never honored this desire? If you aren't leveraging the future to create compelling reasons to choose to move forward every day then you are subconsciously stuck in the here and now.

  You may be snuggling up with the comfy of the status quo, with no compelling vision or desire to go through

167

the inevitable discomfort of change. Reconnecting consciously to your why allows you to get back into the energy of the pull forward instead of having to push yourself forward. The push sucks. You deserve better than that. Create a compelling why that lights you up and pulls you forward with excitement and passion, purpose and joy.

+ **Do you have specific goals set up for each desire?** What are some incremental, tangible goals you can create that might help you walk toward what you want? How are you scheduling deadlines and benchmarks for these goals? Are they written down? Are they on your calendar? Do other people know about your desires and deadlines? Have you enlisted people who will hold you accountable for taking action to move toward your desires?

  If you don't have things written down yet, if they aren't on your calendar, if they are yet to be scheduled out with deadlines, and if no one even knows about your desires, then it's a pretty epic clue that you may think you are committed but in fact are not. It's probably pretty likely that you're just doing busy work to make yourself feel like you are in action. Really, you are caught up in distraction. Truth bomb.

+ **What would it even look like to be all in?** You may not have ever even consciously explored this. Again, if you don't know what you are creating, how can you begin to create it? So explore that consciously now. What might "All In" on this desire look like? What would someone who was all in on this desire be doing? What would they not be doing?

✦ **What are some things you may be able to stop doing** to be in more alignment with what you are saying you desire?

✦ **What are some things you could start doing** to be in even more alignment with what you are saying you desire?

✦ **What are the creative ways you are distracting yourself from committing fully to this desire?** What are your go-to daily distraction activities? Consider: How might you be able to eliminate some of those distractions? What are the backup plans that keep you from really going for it? How might you show up differently if you let go of your backup plans? What are some actions you can take to move you in the direction of shedding those backup plans and committing fully to the actual desires that you have?

✦ **What are you committed to?** In every action that you take or do not take, ask yourself: What does this action tell me I am committed to? For example, if you watch a lot of TV, chances are you are committed to distraction, numbing, and the comfort of the status quo. Be honest with yourself. Bring awareness to how you are choosing distractions over dreams.

✦ **What might be some of the actions that would show you just how committed you are to each of the desires you wrote down?** Pick three things right now that you are committed to doing to move you toward what you want. Write them down. Put them on your calendar. Schedule them. Tell someone about them. Make it real. You deserve to turn your dreams into reality. Take your power back. Make it happen.

If you want to get back to forward movement in the direction of your deepest desires, it is going to be imperative that you explore the subconscious blocks that are getting in your way. Continually assess what you need to start doing and or stop doing so that you can finally give yourself the gift of truly making a decision of desire and genuinely commit to it fully.

Decide Ahead of Time

You need to know what, specifically, you are committing to ahead of time. You need to know what you're willing to work through ahead of time. If not, you'll be trying to make a decision about what to do in the midst of the shitstorms of blocks, resistance, and plenty of opportunities to choose sabotage, distraction, and numbing over commitment to your dreams.

So decide ahead of time.

Power Play

Take out a pen and your journal. Take some time to consider these questions that will help you decide ahead of time.

✦ What **blocks** do you anticipate coming up as you follow each desire?

✦ What is your **agreement with yourself** about how you are going to face each block as is arises? Decide ahead of time.

✦ What may be some things that **could go wrong** and cause you to get triggered into choosing illusionary comfort over desire?

Alignment

Again, it all starts with you. It is your responsibility to know what you want. And it is your responsibility to be in alignment with your own desires. You cannot control or change the world around you, but you sure as shit can shift yourself into whatever direction you want to go. You just need to know where that is.

What direction do you want to move in?

You can't change the past, but you can choose to stop being at the effect of it and finally step into being the Master Creator of your future. That begins now.

It's like the situation with my ex: at first we were on the same page with what we wanted. However, as I learned how to tap into the Power Source of Desire, it started to become more and more clear that we were in wildly different ballparks in terms of what we wanted in life. There were many times over the years that I tried to fit into what his desire template for a relationship was, but it never felt like it was enough for me.

I have learned over the years that when you suppress desire, it just shifts into resentment, anger, and frustration with yourself and your partner. And then it literally oozes out of you everywhere you go. When I finally stepped out of the denial of my own deepest desires, I realized that what I wanted and craved was not in alignment with what he wanted.

At first I accidentally shamed his desires. I no longer wanted to suppress my desire for an Epic and Legendary Life, so I began hoping that he would see that my dreams were amazing and his dreams sucked. I just wanted him to get on board my epic train. (Oopsie! My bad!) A very low vibration part of me wanted him to contort to my desires as I had contorted to his for years. OY VEY! Oh, radical honesty with self can be painful at first, eh?

It took me a long time to realize that he wasn't wrong; he just had a different desire path than me. I wasn't right, and he wasn't wrong. We just weren't in alignment. When I stopped ignoring my responsibility for my own desires, my whole life transformed. I stopped walking through life trying to contort myself like a circus performer to fit into whatever boxes others had created for their desires. I started to create my own damn world. And so can you!

The realization with my ex helped me see the importance of aligned desire paths in a partnership, which allows you to work together in a direction that feeds both souls without either one having to sacrifice dreams or desires—or happiness—for the other. This is one of the coolest things about consciously exploring your desires. When you do, you then get to consciously select partners (romantic, friends, business, etc.) who are in alignment with what you want.

True Power is about knowing what you are responsible for and then taking full responsibility for that through action and alignment. You are responsible for the alignment or misalignment you have with your own desires. The thoughts you think, the words you say, who you surround yourself with, what you do and don't do, the choices you make every moment of every day... they are all either aligning you with forward movement toward where you want to go or they are stalling you and sabotaging your ability to step into your desire Power Source.

Power Play

It's time to get really honest with yourself here. Get out your journal and pen and let's take your conscious alignment to a whole new level. Pick your top three desires and explore alignment. You can revisit this exercise at any point with any desire. This Power Play will help you come into more and more of your power with every desire that emerges.

✦ What are you doing that is **in alignment** with what you want?

✦ What are you doing that is **not in alignment**?

✦ What would **being in alignment** with your words look like? What would you say consistently if you were truly in alignment with the desire? What would you talk about? What would you stop talking about?

✦ What would you focus your **thoughts** on if you were in alignment with your true desires? What thoughts would you stop letting run wild in your head if you were truly in alignment with your desires?

✦ What **actions** would you take on a consistent basis if you were in alignment? What actions would you stop doing?

✦ What are the **new choices** you would like to commit to so that you will be in even more alignment with your desire?

Power of Choice: Leveraging "I Choose"

Whenever I go to make a decision or I can feel myself about to take an action step that is not in alignment with what I want, I ask myself, "What do you choose?" This question helps me hold myself accountable for choosing the action. If I choose comfort, fear, distraction, or numbing, then I have an agreement to be honest with myself about it.

With honesty comes some really beautiful opportunities to get curious and explore the truths about what I am afraid of as I contemplate stepping into even more desire and even more power. Remember to give yourself permission to choose honesty and curiosity without the side of shame. So in the moments where you are faced with an opportunity to align yourself with your desires, use "I choose." It is so powerful as it allows you to know that you get to make the choice about which direction you move. Whether you choose the familiarity of mediocrity and contorting to other people's desires or whether you choose to honor you, it is all a choice. You are the sole Power Source of all choices you make. Be sure to celebrate yourself when you choose alignment.

On the days where I feel pulled to choose comfort and sabotage but I choose to work out, I repeat the following mantra over and over again as I am working out. It helps me take my power back.

TAKE YOUR POWER BACK!

I choose an epic and legendary life.
I choose to nourish my body. I choose to be
strong. I choose to move in the direction of my
dreams. I choose to make time for myself.

#powerfulAF

Try it out for yourself. Celebrate all the ways you are choosing epic and legendary. I cannot wait to see all the epicness that you choose for yourself!

The Power of Patterns

Finally, as we wrap up our powerful desire exploration, pay attention to your own patterns that show up. As you have completed each of these Power Plays what common themes have been revealed in your answers? What keeps repeating over and over? Look for your patterns.

The patterns of desire that you have seen repeating in our work together through this journey are calling to you and asking you to expand. There are no coincidences. Repeating patterns of desire are trying to get your attention. They are urging you to move in a direction of infinite possibility and delight.

Have a little more faith! Trust in yourself and in your desires.

Get crystal clear on what you want and how you are committed to showing up. Decide ahead of time how you will navigate the inevitable blocks that will come up for you. Create clarity of desire so you can truly be the Master Creator of every area of your life.

POWER SOURCE #4

IMAGINATION—A CONDUIT TO INFINITE POSSIBILITY

POWER QUOTE

Imagination is everything. It is the preview of life's coming attractions.
Albert Einstein

It is ironic that something that is one of your most epic Power Sources can also be used against you. It can help you tap into your deepest desires, and it can also lead you to tap into your deepest fears. It can paint your mental canvas with the most vivid pictures of your wildest dreams, and it can absorb the fears swirling around in the world around you. It can be an epic catalyst for forward movement in the direction you crave to go.

It can also be used against you as a means of keeping you "safe"—stuck in the "comfort" of the familiar pains and good enoughs that mediocrity yields. We often allow our imagination to run wild with worst-case scenarios and rarely ever stop to consciously ask, "What is the best thing that might happen?"

Until now.

Power and the Shadow Side of Imagination

We use our imaginations to take ourselves out of pursuing our dreams, imagining the endless paralyzing what ifs. We call it being "safe," "responsible," and "realistic." Then, when it comes to the profound dreams and visions we see, feel, and hear, we discount them as "just my imagination," "make believe," and "not realistic."

Well, I hate to break it to the diehard skeptics who like to stay rooted in "reality," but if the dreams and visions are "made up," then so are all of your hypothetical what ifs. All those what ifs that are stopping you from stepping into your dreams are really just your imagination. The truth is you're settling for mediocrity.

On top of that, you've been justifying your settling by convincing yourself that the best use of your imagination is to dream up all those creative what ifs and "plan ahead" to prevent the worst. Meanwhile, I and many others are over here leveraging the power side of imagination to create an unshakable and relentless belief in self and consciously cultivating space for the magic of intuition, visions, and dreams. I invite you to join me, my friend.

If at any point you hear yourself saying anything similar to, "It's too risky to chase x, y, z dream," I challenge you to dig deeper. Too risky based on what? Based on all the what ifs? What are the "facts" that go with those what ifs? Often times your Ninja Mind presents facts based on hearsay and secondhand information:

- ✓ *"Well, this one time…"*
- ✓ *"X happened to so and so…"*
- ✓ *"I read this article once that said…"* *
- ✓ *"Blah blah blah statistics say…"*

* Insert the name of any TV program, video, or any other source that's not actually firsthand experience.

My favorite excuse is when the Ninja Mind uses something that happened one time only, as if that one time you gave it a real go and now you should just accept that dreams are for those other people who must somehow have it all figured out. They must be some kind of anomaly, eh? Must be nice for them.

OK, well then, with that same logic isn't it also true that there is proof of success for you in your life as well? What are the moments where you risked the what ifs and something positive came as a result? If you answered something to the effect that there are no examples in your own life and you have some sort of excuse or justification that supports you staying where you are in your nice, sweet, familiar "comfort" zone, then you are all sorts of married to the shadow side of your imagination—and very committed to the struggle.

Let's just acknowledge that the commitment to the struggle is a choice. This is where radical honesty with yourself comes in to play.

TAKE YOUR POWER BACK!

What are you really committed to?
What are you choosing? Dreams?
Or comfort masked as safety, playing it
smart, and being realistic?

#powerfulAF

Let me give you an example. I was on a plane heading to L.A. and began a conversation with the gentleman sitting next to me. The topic of dreams came up, and we started to explore his. He kept saying, "What if I take the leap and start my business and then, 15 years from now, I realize my business wasn't what I wanted it to be, and then my kids can't go to college...." I mirrored back, "It sounds like you are exercising your creativity and imagination to create the worst-case scenario. Let's be equally generous and fair with your imagination skills and play out the answer to, "What's the best-case scenario?""

His eyes got big. He had spent so much time exercising the shadow side of imagination and sabotaging his dreams that he had never consciously invested in the power side of imagination that had the potential to fuel his dreams.

So let's do that for you and your dreams, shall we?

Power Play

Take out a pen and your journal. Let's explore the infinite possibilities of shifting from the shadow side of imagination to the power side of it.

+ Where in your life are you currently leveraging the **power of imagination** to help fuel your dreams?

+ What are some areas of your life and or specific instances where you might be **falling into the power trap** of the shadow side of imagination? For each instance explore this question: *What is the shadow side of imagination trying to protect you from?* There is always some benefit that you are getting when you choose fear over dreams.

  Get conscious on what the benefit is each time the shadow pattern shows up. To do that, ask yourself: *What are you so afraid of in giving yourself permission to choose your dreams?* The next question I asked the guy on the plane was this: "And what if 15 years go by and you never even gave yourself a chance to choose your dreams because you were so busy letting fear rule you? What then?" Ask yourself the same question right now. See what comes up for you.

✦ When you look at your **actions, decisions, choices, and behaviors** in every area of life as either in alignment with your true dreams and desires or in alignment with your fears, what do you see?

  ✓ *What are some ways that you are committed to your dreams in your life right now?*

  ✓ *And what are some ways you are showing yourself that you are committed to your comfort and your fears?*

  ✓ *What might it look like to be committed fully to your dreams?*

✦ If you were to give yourself permission to play even more in the **power side of imagination** how might you do that? For example, I do Dream Journaling where I ask myself:

  ✓ *What would blow my own damn mind?*

✓ *What would excite and delight the everliving shit out of me to get to learn, experience, or create?*

✓ *What do I really want to experience most—in life, in love, in business, with friends and family?*

I also do dream jams with friends. I ask them to journal their dreams and I journal mine, then we talk about them. I am always so inspired when I hear another person's dreams and it ignites me to dream even bigger.

I share exercises and ideas in my book *Epic Sexy You: No Limits. No Rules.* If you are loving the Power Plays in this book and want even more soulful and expansive goodies, make sure to get a copy of that book as well.

The Power of Being an Imagination Conduit

Your intuition is the epic Power Source where your grand visions, epic ideas, powerful dreams, divine guidance and messages reside. Often times intuition gets dismissed as "just your imagination" or mistaken for just another thought flying through your mind. Your Ninja Mind will demand an explanation—a logical reason for doing whatever it is that you are feeling pulled to do. Yet, often with intuition you don't have a reason other than "it feels right." You can't explain. You "just *know.*"

When you say yes to the visions and ideas that the universe delivers through the whispers of your intuition, you are always given more. If, however, you dismiss any of what you are given, it's then given to someone else. Have you ever had an idea and didn't pull it through, but then you watched someone else pull it through and magic unfolded in their life as a result?

You are a channel receiving the frequency of creation. If you remain open and take action, more comes through. You can turn it on or off and up or down, based on how much you are in alignment with whatever path you're being guided to. I'm over here like a fire hose of soul creations because I take action on what I'm given. I have embraced being the Master Creator and so can you.

Take action. Follow the path of your desires and dreams.

Power Play

To tap the power side of imagination and paint your dreams, you can access your intuition by grabbing a journal and pen, sitting still and asking yourself the following questions. Listen with your heart to hear the whispers that are there to guide you to the path that is right for you. Then commit to taking little actions consistently to move you toward honoring your heart, even if reason and logic evade you. When you do, watch your whole life transform.

Are you ready?

✦ What have you been **hearing whispered to you** repeatedly in the past few months and or perhaps even the past few years of your life? What is something you can do to start taking action on those whispers today?

✦ What do you **know you need to do** but haven't done so yet? What is one step you can take to move yourself forward?

✦ What do you **know you need to stop doing** but haven't done it yet? What is one step you can take to move yourself in the direction of stopping what is getting in the way of your desires?

✦ What is something that you **know will help you move forward** in your life but you haven't committed to it yet? What would committing to it fully look like? What is one step you can take to move yourself more into that commitment?

When you catch yourself in the shadow side of imagination, lost in the land of the paralyzing what ifs, shift yourself into the power side of imagination by asking these three questions:

✓ *What are all of the best-case scenarios that might happen?*

✓ *What if it all worked out?*

✓ *What if it's the best thing ever?*

When your Ninja Mind demands a logical reason and you don't have one, go into your memory bank. Show the Ninja Mind the moments in your past where you chose to go with intuition over the logic. Consciously harvest and highlight all the positive things that happened as a result.

Choose to leverage the power of your imagination. You are so worth that dream life. Get it! Bet on you!

POWER SOURCE #5

THE ALCHEMY OF FEAR: TRANSMUTE FEAR INTO POWER

POWER QUOTE

Make a radical change in your lifestyle and begin to boldly do things which you may previously never have thought of doing, or been too hesitant to attempt. So many people live within unhappy circumstances and yet will not take the initiative to change their situation because they are conditioned to a life of security, conformity, and conservation, all of which may appear to give one peace of mind, but in reality nothing is more damaging to the adventurous spirit within a man than a secure future. The very basic core of a man's living spirit is his passion for adventure. The joy of life comes from our encounters with new experiences, and hence there is no greater joy than to have an endlessly changing horizon, for each day to have a new and different sun. If you want to get more out of life, you must lose your inclination for monotonous security and adopt a helter-skelter style of life that will at first appear to you to be crazy. But once you become accustomed to such a life you will see its full meaning and its incredible beauty.
Jon Krakauer, *Into the Wild*

185

Your personal relationship with fear is either going to be one in which you are anchoring your power in or one in which you are hemorrhaging power as fast as blood flowing from a direct cut of a main artery. If you fear it, you will give it more power. If you avoid and or ignore fear, you will give it more power. If you focus on your fears or on what you don't want, then you are giving those things more power. If fear has the power, you do not.

If, however, you feel the fear and do it anyway, you dance with your dreams. You face the very thing you are afraid of. You do the very thing you don't feel "ready" to do. You allow fear to come along for the ride but make it sit in the back seat while your dreams and courage take the wheel. When you do this, you will uncover one of the most profound sources of power—a sustainable, unshakable power that can fuel your dreams.

POWER QUOTE

The cave you fear to enter
holds the treasure you seek.
Joseph Campbell

Fear Is the Birthplace of a New You

You need to decide ahead of time what your relationship to and agreement with fear is going to be. If you do not make this clear choice in advance, you will default to letting fear take the wheel. If you wait to make agreements and negotiate with fear as it is presented to you, you will notice a pattern where your subconscious mind lures you into choosing comfort over dreams. "Tomorrow sounds real good for that dream opportunity," your Ninja Mind will tell you, "but today we're going to pass."

Oh hey, Ninja Mind! Let's choose comfort just this once, eh? Even though we know damn well that it is never "just this one time." My own personal upfront agreement with fear is that when it emerges I lean in. When something comes up and I don't feel "ready" to take on that opportunity or challenge, I say yes. I lean in to the stretch and dance with my fear.

I choose to snuggle with my inner demons instead of ignoring them and letting them rule me. I'm all, "Come here, you cute little limiting belief. Let's cuddle and talk about it!"

I have become known for these agreements with myself. It puts me in some interesting situations, and it invites others into epic stretch moments as well. From skydiving to swimming with sharks, from writing books that air all of my darkness to the entire world to bungee jumping off one of the highest bridges in the world, from a five-day mountaineering trip (that involved a glacier, mountain goats, and a couple of toenails lost) to walking with lions in South Africa, epic adventure is the name of my game.

One day about four years ago I received an invitation to fear. A friend of a friend reached out and said that he had learned I was coming to their town. He had heard a rumor about my agreement with myself to face my fears, so he invited me to join him on stage at a stand-up comedy open mic.

I was immediately flooded with fear and resistance.

Right before I could get an excuse out of my mouth, a little intuitive whisper reminded me of my upfront agreement with myself. I reluctantly said yes and then spent the next few weeks subconsciously leveraging the shadow side of my imagination. I dreamed up all the ways I could get myself out of the agreement.

As the event got nearer, my worst-case scenario stories got more and more creative. One of my favorite and most ridiculous stories that I made up was when I envisioned the audience throwing tomatoes at me. I had had enough of my own stalling tactics by that point. I leaned in. I decided to commit and be all in.

On the day of the event, I was still terrified and freaking out. I kept reminding myself that the intersection of terrifying and exhilarated is where the most epic growth exists. I was mentally pumping myself up and trying to remember to breathe as the emcee took the stage. He said, "What you will notice on the tables in front of you are tomatoes. We ask that if someone sucks you boo them and throw the tomatoes at them."

Whaaaaat??? Wait... WHAT???!!

I shit you not. I cannot make this up! Now, granted, they were not actual tomatoes; they were foam tomatoes. But even I hadn't thought about the fact that they would boo me while I was up there. This was a unicorn—a rarity of a sighting in life where the worst-case scenario is actually worse than the wildest imagining of worst-case scenarios.

I had to keep reminding myself to breathe. I could feel my frontal cortex going offline continuously, and I had to keep trying to get it to come back on. As defined by Wikipedia, the frontal cortex is the part of the brain that is responsible for functions such as "planning for the future, judgment, decision making skills, attention span, and inhibition." You don't need to know the terminology. You just need to know that I was freaking the f*ck out!!! The only thing keeping me sane was knowing that soon I could take the stage and have my turn. Then it would be over.

Four hours later, the second-to-last person of the evening to take the stage was me. Man, when life wants to gift you growth it sure does go big, eh?! I had to keep calming down the mind chatter swirling inside my head. I had to fight myself continuously for four hours to not fall prey to the endless excuses that plagued me as to why I should leave. One of my favorite excuses that the Ninja Mind chatter offered up was that I could just leave and never speak to any of these people ever again.

The guy who had invited me was a friend of a friend. I didn't technically know him. Everyone else I had just met, so I could just drop off the face of the planet and problem solved! Yay for Ninja Mind solutions! Except for one incredibly important detail that was missing from that "solution." If I had left, *I* would have known about it, and I would not have been proud of Who I showed up as that day. So I stayed, surviving the battle between my head and heart for those four hours.

I took the stage and blacked out. Not literally like back in my drinking days. In fact, on this day I was stone cold sober due to my commitment to live life fully present. But, figuratively, I blacked out. I did my piece, and then I got off that stage as quickly as I could. I had no idea how to gauge what had happened other than celebrating that there were no tomatoes thrown and no one booed me. But what happened next caught me so off guard. It changed my life forever.

The gentleman who took the stage after me said, "Well, ladies and gentlemen, she may not be a comedian, but she sure is one of the best public speakers I've ever seen."

Wait, what? What did he just say? Who was he talking about? Me? Public speaker? What? Whaaaaat??

Later I watched the video that the friend of the friend had recorded. Sure as shit, you couldn't even tell how nervous I was. In fact, I even appeared to be having a lot of fun and looked super comfortable on stage. My mind was blown.

In that moment, a public speaker was born.

Why am I sharing this story with you? Because your Ninja Mind will have you believe that you need to become a version of you first, in order to be "ready" to step into opportunities that come your way. The actual truth is that you become a new version of you by doing the shit that you do not feel "ready" to do. You grow with confidence and expand into a more unshakable and powerful version of you by doing the very thing you are afraid of.

Walking into fear is the birthplace of the new reference points that you need in order to become the new version of you that you are craving to uplevel into. Although vision work is a powerful tool, you cannot merely think yourself into a new version of you. Although reading is also a powerful tool, you cannot merely read books and study your way into an upgraded identity.

You have to do the work. You cannot pay someone else to do it for you. I can assure you, absolutely nothing is a substitute for the action of facing your fears and *feeling* your way into experiencing new versions of you.

Power Play

Take out a pen and your journal, and let's rock!

✦ What are some things you are **feeling pulled to do** and yet you are afraid of them?

✦ If you were to take a page out of Grant Cardone's **The 10x Rule**, and you were to multiply your courage by 10 times the amount that it currently is, what would you start doing? If you were to 10x your courage, what would you stop doing? If you were to 10x your courage, what would you continue doing but shift or tweak it to allow it to be even more powerful?

✦ What are you **afraid to do** that you know, when you do it, will blow your own mind?

✦ When was the last time you tried **something new** for the very first time?

✦ When was the last time you did **something that really scares you**?

✦ What is **one thing you are going to commit to DO** so you can get new reference points for what you are capable of doing? Pick one thing at a time and do it. Then pay close attention as your whole life transforms.

✦ What are the reference points from your **past moments of courage** that you can pull on when fear pops up? Every time fear kicks in for me, I return to a few key reference points. I am like, "Hey, remember that one time that beyond your worst-case-scenario thing happened where the audience was encouraged to throw tomatoes at you and boo if you sucked, and you did it anyway? Remember in that moment when a public speaker was born? I wonder what else kind of magic we can find when we snuggle with our demons and dance with our fears?"

Pick one thing, do it, and watch your entire identity shift on the other side of the experience. And, remember, you get out of this journey what you put into it. Bet on you!

POWER QUOTE

Your life unfolds in direct proportion to your courage.
Danielle LaPorte

The Intersection of Desire, Empowerment, and Safety

There are moments in life where you will be tempted to create "safety" for yourself in ways that actually keep you from the magic of this divine world. Find the courage and consciousness within to choose desire over fear and protection.

For example, my dog Izzy fell into the pool a while back while chasing a squirrel. My immediate reaction was to figure out how to protect her and keep her safe. That led to my mind finding all the ways I could keep her out of the pool—put a gate around the pool, leash her on the other side of the yard, never let her out of the house again. You know, all the logical things one's mind thinks of when in protection mode.

As soon as I caught my fear taking over, I snapped out of my reactionary mode and instead went into a response mode that I've tamed my mind to access. I started to consciously explore what I was doing. I quickly realized I was trying to draw safety boundaries for her from a place of fear instead of a place of expansion desire and love.

So I asked myself, "What are the possibilities I've been missing because I was trying to create safety from fear? What are the possibilities for creating safety from a higher vibration of true empowerment?" Right then and there, boom, I heard: "Teach her how to swim." The answer was waiting for me the moment I decided to go within.

She struggled. She didn't like it. Once, she missed the stairs and exhausted herself trying to get out of the pool. A few times she needed help getting out. I let her struggle a little longer than she or I felt comfortable with so she could master this new skill.

For any of you who may be using the shadow side of imagination to think I was putting her at risk to drown, please understand that even a millisecond is uncomfortable to watch someone you love fight to learn something new. I was standing right there next to her in the event that she actually did need me, but I gave her enough space for the gift of her own discomfort. So, please, breathe and come back to the lesson with me.

Your calm and loving presence with someone you love who is in the midst of a metamorphosis struggle actually sends them the message that you believe they are strong enough on their own. You not jumping in to do the work for them sends them a big "you've got this" vote of confidence. So, please, check yo' anxiety boo.

Even though the last pool lesson of the day was epic and she found the stairs immediately, I knew she was going to need more lessons, more time, and more attempts in order for her to get the hang of it and sustain her growth. It's an ongoing journey, and I'm on board for that ride. I love her enough to allow her the space to learn, which includes letting her be uncomfortable and figure it out for herself.

I'm sharing this story with you for you to hit pause and consciously explore these questions:

✦ Where are you **drawing boundaries** from a place of fear?

✦ Where are you trying to **keep yourself and others safe** and calling it "love" when really it's just fear?

✦ Where are you **depriving others** of the discomfort of learning for themselves because it makes you so uncomfortable to see them so uncomfortable?

✦ Where are you **feeling responsible** for another person's struggles or thinking they can't do it for themselves?

When you're in that vibration of fear, you may find yourself stuck in a pattern of stepping in to "help" but, despite your good intentions, you actually end up disrupting the struggle, which as you know is the final, majestic stage of the metamorphosis process that is preparing their wings to fly. When you interject yourself here, you disrupt all of the learning available to them in this phase. Even though you're not intending to, you're sending the message to them that you don't think they are strong enough or smart enough to do it on their own.

✓ *How is this pattern showing up in your life?*

✓ *How are you doing this to others?*

✓ *And how might you be doing this to yourself?*

TAKE YOUR POWER BACK!

Disrupting growth and expansion in the name of "love" and being "helpful" when someone has not asked you for help is really just your fear and epic discomfort getting in the way of growth and expansion—yours and theirs.

#powerfulAF

Power Play

Take out a pen and your journal, and let's rock!

✦ What are some areas of your own life where you may be **subconsciously operating from fear** and protection instead of desire?

✦ How might you **show up differently** if you genuinely believed others were strong enough to do their soul work for themselves?

✦ What are the **possibilities you've potentially been missing out on** because you were trying to create safety from fear?

✦ What are some **possibilities for creating safety** from a higher vibration of true empowerment and desire? What might that look like? Play with tangible examples in your own life where this is showing up. Find new ways of creating safety that are in alignment with you as a powerful, playful being and Master Creator of your life.

When you catch yourself in old patterns of creating safety by giving in to the voice of fear, take your power back. Ask yourself: *How might safety, desire, love, true empowerment, and delight co-exist and dance together to create even more magical possibilities for me in this very moment in my life?* Boom. Back in a space of desire, empowerment, safety, and possibility!

Beware the "Must Be Nice" and "Anomaly" Syndromes

I have found that the more awakened I become, the more epic shit that I do, the more I love being me, and the more I live the most dope life of all time, the more I hear people say things like, "Must be nice," "You're so fearless," and "Well, yeah, but you're an anomaly." It's as if they see my power, happiness, and self love, my knowingness of who I am, and the epic life of dream chasing that I live and they think that somehow I have something they don't have. They think I must not experience fear like they do.

What they are neglecting to acknowledge is the time and energy I put in and the fears I faced. They don't see the epic learning curves and the wildly uncomfortable moments of my growth journey where I chose to lean in rather than shrink back. They forget to consider how I bet on me even when no one else could see my vision. They don't know that I had faith even in the darkness. Or that I chose dreams over comfort consistently and persistently.

196

Sometimes when people hear that I was making $250K before I took a leap into entrepreneurship, their response is, "Well then, you wouldn't understand where I'm at..." Insert whatever job they are in and any and all BS excuses their Ninja Mind is making up to justify and rationalize why they are holding on for dear life to their comfort zone when they deserve so much more.

It's just fear though. I get it! It's scary as shit to let go of the certainty of what is familiar and known. We all have "logical" reasons to stay in the status quo, even though deep down we know we are not truly living. We know we are meant for so much more. Damn those logical reasons and the Ninja Mind.

I had 250 thousand reasons to stay at that job. Do you know how much courage it took to leave 250 thousand logical reasons to stay? Not to mention all the other perks and benefits of the job that made it super alluring for me to stay and choose "comfort" over my dreams—the 401K, epic health benefits, job security, company card, travel all over the US and all-expenses paid trips to exotic destinations, epic business events, and more.

If I was broke as hell leaving the corporate world to start my own business would that have somehow required more courage from me? Or if I was making $30K would that have been more courageous to leave?

All of those versions require courage. All of them.

Some people's Ninja Minds have even said to me that I could potentially be perceived as bragging when I share the numbers and the specifics of all the perks. Dear Ninja Mind, why the hell would I brag about leaving something that people literally thought I was batshit crazy to leave?

I look back at that time in my life when I finally put in my notice and decided to leave. Most people around me thought I had lost my mind. I am not kidding. I could feel people questioning whether there was something wrong with me. They were concerned for my mental health. People were literally questioning my ability to make rational decisions.

It's kind of funny, now that I can see how deeply our subconscious minds are programmed for conforming to fears and following the masses. We often think it's literally crazy when someone takes the leap and trusts that they will figure out how to fly on their way down.

Thank God for consciously reprogramming, eh?!

After I took the leap, leaving the corporate life, what "work" looked like became wildly different from the norm you see in society. "Work" became getting paid to take a group of ladies bungee jumping, skydiving, and or lounging in the sun while experiencing soulfully expansive life altering life coaching. "Work" became snuggling koalas in Australia, icepick climbing in Iceland, snowmobiling on a glacier, a jungle swing in Costa Rica, ziplining in Mexico, and swimming with sharks. These days I welcome guests into my retreat house for custom immersion weekends here in Miami and I have an outdoor office by the pool.

Before you think, "Oh, must be nice" or your Ninja Mind tries to tell you that I am an anomaly, I'd like to remind you that I put in the work and made my version of joy happen. It started with identifying that the way I used to "work" didn't feel aligned with the joy factory and epic, soulful, divine being that I am. When I came to that realization, I sat still and committed myself to exploring this question: "Well, what do I want?"

Do you notice that that question is the thread weaving this book together? What do you want? You cannot create something without knowing very clearly what it is that you want. Fuzzy targets do not get hit.

On my way to my epic and legendary life, I tried on a ton of things to feel my way through desire until I got crystal clear on what I wanted. I wanted to make a living by working from anywhere in the world. I decided I wanted to be able to do powerful soul work in amazingly luxurious and divine spaces.

I wanted to have an outdoor office and get to work in a bikini, sitting in the sun beside a majestic pool. I wanted to make a living while living. For me, adventure is the heartbeat of existence, and I wanted to make a living while experiencing all that this playground of a world has to offer. I decided these things. I committed fully to my desires. I braved the discomfort and the unknown. Epic changes that were required for me to make this happen.

Consider that your resistance to my success or anyone else's is simply your Ninja Mind's attempt to talk yourself out of why "working" can't be more joyous for you too. Know that your version of joy may not look like mine. What do you want?

I left an incredibly lucrative, comfy and fluffy, highly sought after, prestigious position in my corporate job to start my own business. I left a relationship with someone I loved and cared for deeply. Despite our connection, I had to be radically honest with myself that he was not in alignment with the life I wanted. And I was no longer in alignment with the life he wanted.

I left my hometown, which I love, and moved across the country to Miami, where I didn't really know anyone very well. I sold or donated almost everything I owned, and I started over. I let go of the old, shredded my comfort blanket, and trusted that the new would arrive.

And it has! It's even better than I ever could have imagined. Fortune truly does favor the bold and all souls who have the courage to bet on themselves. If I can do it, so can you.

So, before you look at how I live my life and say, "Must be nice," or "Yeah, but you're an anomaly," or count yourself out thinking that somehow I must be different from you, just remember that that's just your Ninja Mind. That part of you genuinely thinks its sole job is to keep you safe. Therefore, it subconsciously assassinates your greatness and puts your dreams on hold for a tomorrow that never comes.

That part of you knows how much courage it takes to chase your dreams and brave the unknown. It knows how risky it might be to trust that it will all work out in your favor. That part of you does not want you to do the work, because it does not want you to grow. I am not an anomaly. I am courageous AF (as f*ck). If you'd just give yourself a little more credit, bet on you, and take some steps toward your dreams, you'll see what you're actually capable of too. This book is an invitation to step into your own profound courage and greatness.

Be aware that saying, "Must be nice," or "You are so fearless!" is also insulting to the person on the receiving end of your Ninja Mind's limiting beliefs. Those beliefs, which you are projecting onto them, are insinuating that their Power came naturally. It discounts all that they did to get themselves to where they are now and it ignores all that they continue to do to keep themselves moving forward.

The next time you catch yourself thinking or saying, "Must be nice," or writing someone off as some kind of "anomaly" as a way of convincing yourself that you'll never get where you want to go, just realize that your Ninja Mind is trying to make you feel better for playing small. Just stop. Get honest with yourself. Say, "Thats a lot of work." Or, "I want that, and need to change my relationship with fear in order to have that." If you're going to play small or choose fear at least be honest with yourself about it.

Stop BYOB (Buying Your Own Bullshit). Be honest with yourself. Take your power back. If I can do it, so can you. You're so damn worth it, and you are so much more powerful than you can even imagine. Bet on you. Create your heaven on earth. Invest in your dreams.

Take the leaps—or take baby steps to move you in the direction you want to grow in. Go at whatever pace will allow you to move forward and show fear that it is not the boss of you. Feel the fear and do it anyway. Take breaks and take naps. Get all up in those fear meltdowns. Fall down, get back up, fall down again. Just never quit on you.

POWER QUOTE

I learned that courage was not the absence of fear, but the triumph over it. The brave man is not he who does not feel afraid, but he who conquers that fear.
Nelson Mandela

POWER SOURCE #6

BECOME A BADASS AT FAILURE & PERSISTENCE

POWER QUOTE

Our greatest glory in life is not in our never falling, but in rising up every time we fall.
Ralph Waldo Emerson

Let's normalize what happens in the process of expansion, awakening, and learning. First, know this: you will inevitably fail. You will bump into things you do not know how to do. You will doubt yourself. You may turn into a two-year-old child, and yet when you persist through it all you will grow. It's like Henry Ford says, "Failure is the opportunity to begin again more intelligently." With every failure comes buttloads of lessons that you can harvest and extrapolate to consciously create even more magic, abundance, and thriving in your life.

However, if there is nothing currently in your life that is requiring persistence, then you are playing life safe. By "safe," I mean that you are not truly stepping into your fullest potential of the magical, juicy living you came here to experience. Not experiencing failure means you are living inside that super warm and cozy comfort zone.

The comfort zone is anything but safe. It is the place where the best you're ever going to experience is "good." It is a place where no growth happens, where greatness does not exist, and where epic and legendary are nowhere to be found. If you are not growing, you're not truly living.

Unfortunately, along with the pandemic of accepting mediocrity, there is another widespread and dangerous phenomenon running rampant in our society. I call it the *Shortcut Pandemic*. This is when you want the learning and the growth and all of the epic goodies on the other side of the stretch zone *without* having to do the work.

That's right, you want to skip right to the muscle and see results *without* doing the workouts. You'd like to bypass exercising your persistence muscle and avoid failure altogether.

That is not how this epic and legendary living thing works. This book is chock full of ways you can construct your own paradigm of powerful living and create a life beyond your wildest dreams. But you will have to work for it. You will have to be persistent like a mofo.

You cannot outsource the work. That is a promise. You have to bet on you every single step of the way *and* learn to have an epic relationship with the raw truths of growth and expansion. All of that includes dancing with the inevitability of failure.

Power Play

Get your journal and pen out! Let's leave mediocrity in the dust and play with shifting your relationship with failure and persistence to an even more empowering one, shall we? Make sure to write your answers out. Explore where the biggest opportunities for growth are awaiting you.

✦ If you are being radically honest with yourself, what are the areas in your life where you are **failing to show up fully** and courageously?

✦ Where in life are you being required to **lean in to persistence** in order to keep moving forward?

✦ What are each of the moments of failure and persistence **teaching you**? How are they gifts for you on your journey towards your deepest desires and dreams?

✦ How might these experiences be **happening _for_ you**?

✦ You can even go back into the past and harvest lessons learned. What were **past failures** trying to teach you? What were the gifts that perhaps you couldn't see at the time but you now see? When you find the lessons and gifts of past perceived "failures," you can literally rewrite history. You can transmute the energy of failure and step onto a playground of possibility. There, you can go treasure hunting for new learning and have an attitude of gratitude about all you have experienced so far on your life's journey.

✦ How are you giving yourself a proactive, conscious, and intentional **opportunity to fail**?

✦ What are some **new areas of life** where you would like to give yourself a proactive, conscious, and intentional opportunity to fail?

Your Relationship with Failure

POWER QUOTE

*My dad encouraged us to fail.
Growing up he would ask us what we failed
at that week. If we didn't have something he would
be disappointed. It changed my mindset
at an early age that failure is not the outcome,
failure is not trying. Don't be afraid to fail.*
Sara Blakely, billionaire and founder of Spanx

POWER QUOTE

*I've missed more than 9,000 shots in my career.
I've lost almost 300 games. 26 times I've been
trusted to take the game winning shot and missed.
I've failed over and over and over again in my
life. And that is why I succeed.*
Michael Jordan

Power Play

What is your relationship with and definition of failure?
Failure is often seen as:

    ✓ *Not having the courage to try at all.*

    ✓ *Not experiencing the outcome you were aiming for.*

Instead of feeling the illusionary permanence that fear may try to get you to buy into when you experience failure, consider another option. See it all as a playground of growth and infinite opportunity for expansion. Failure is a magical land of harvesting new learning for creating even more powerfully on your next attempt at whatever you are striving to master. Failure truly is a gift. You just have to be courageous enough to lean in and accept what it has to offer you.

What if, instead of avoiding failure, you celebrated every single juicy yummy failure you experienced? And, if you haven't failed a lot, what if you gave yourself the gift of consciously creating even more things in your life to grow and stretch into, so that you can get to experience all of the powerful learning that is in every inevitable bump that you encounter along the way?

- ✦ Every day ask, what have I *failed at today?* What did I learn from each perceived failure? What is each failure teaching me? What were the gifts and the blessings in each failure that will help me move forward and be an even more powerful me in the future? How might each failure be happening *for* me and in service to my epic growth and expansion?

- ✦ Every week ask, what have I *failed at this week?* What did I learn from each perceived failure? What is each one teaching me? What were the gifts and the blessings in each failure that will help me move forward and be an even more powerful me in the future? How might each failure be happening *for* me and in service to my epic growth and expansion?

✦ Every month ask, what have I *failed at this month?* What did I learn from each perceived failure? What is each one teaching me? What were the gifts and the blessings in each failure that will help me move forward and be an even more powerful me in the future? How might each one of these failures be happening *for* me and in service to my epic growth and expansion?

✦ What are some *disempowering beliefs* that I have about failure? Once you bring these to the surface, you will be more conscious of not BYOB (Buying Your Own Bullshit).

✦ What might be *more empowering beliefs* that I can create about failure and have ready to replace old beliefs when they inevitably pop up and try to stop or stall my growth?

Keep checking in with yourself to make sure you are *consciously creating opportunities* to stretch and grow, to learn and fail. Learn to continually scan for dis-empowering beliefs. Choose to intentionally program new and empowering beliefs that serve you as you continuously move forward in the direction that you want to go.

Consciously Normalize Failure and Commit to Persistence

As we discussed when exploring your desires and your commitment to your dreams, two of the most powerful tools you can employ are to normalize the failure you are sure to encounter and to prioritize persistence. Look ahead and explore:

✦ What are some **blocks** that may come up on the path ahead as you pursue your dreams and desires?

✦ What are some of the **stretch points**?

✦ What are some of the **learning curves**?

Normalize the shitstorms you may face. Decide ahead of time to be all in. For example, if you want epic love, what might be some of the blocks, stretch points, and learning curves you may face? Rejection. Bad dates. Heartbreak. Great dates. Mind blowing connections that go nowhere. Liking someone and it not being reciprocated. Bad timing. Misalignment. Super close, but not a match. Silence. Waiting. No response.

The person you are crazy about may sabotage the connection when things get great. You may sabotage the connection.

When you decide ahead of time that these are normal pieces of the journey, it allows you to not feel so damn blindsided when the inevitable bumps happen. The next time your Ninja Mind is trying to keep you "safe" and wanting to back out every single time something goes wrong, ask yourself these questions:

✓ *What is this trying to teach me?*

✓ *What can I learn from this?*

✓ *What can I tweak for next time?*

✓ *What can I do different next time to create an even more powerful experience?*

These questions will shift your energy and your relationship with learning, persistence, and failure from Victimo / Victima ("This sucks, why bother?") to a more empowered approach that will have you saying, "This is a part of the journey. Game on! What's up next? Let's rock!"

Celebrate your frustration, your stuckness, your confusion, and your "failures" along the way. Remember, when you step outside of your comfort zone, you merely expand it. Those with the most massive comfort zones are those who tend to be the ones living more in one week, month, or year than most will ever live in a lifetime. And it all happens just one tiny step at a time.

What's your one tiny step forward for today?

POWER SOURCE #7

BE A BOSS OF TIME

POWER QUOTE

If you love life, don't waste time,
for time is what life is made up of.
Bruce Lee

Have you ever felt like a day, a month, a year, or decades have blinked by? This was my experience of the first thirty years of my life and especially the years between 20 to 30, when I was sleepwalking like a pro. Time blinking by may be a clue that you are not living wide awake.

The good news is that this entire book is a conduit of consciousness. It is a portal of awakening to living life on purpose. In this section we get to play with how you get to do that when it comes to the time investments that you are making.

Have you ever been curious about why, when we all have the same amount of time in a day, some people literally appear to have more time than others do? The reason for this is linked to the way the time is being invested.

For example, you may have heard the term "compounding" used with regard to finance and investment strategies. The term refers to steady investments made over a period of time, resulting in financial growth. The longer the duration of your investment, the greater return you can expect.

The same is true for time investment strategies. You will either find yourself compounding in the direction of your dreams or slipping back toward the black hole of stuckness and stagnation. This is all great news if you are investing your time consciously in those things that feed your dreams and desires. Not so great news if you are not consciously investing your time or if you are letting your Ninja Mind do the investing for you.

You will have enough time for whatever you decide to consciously make time for. Ironically, we tend to make time for distractions and numbing and then conveniently call it relaxing. Treat yo-self to some numbing and distractions!

WOO!! We are so busy prioritizing "relaxation" that many of us leave our dreams for the tomorrow that never comes. This is not intentional, but it can happen to us all. It is time to take your power back.

What Is Your Relationship to Time?

POWER QUOTE

*A man who dares to waste one hour of time
has not discovered the value of life.*
Charles Darwin

Where does time fall in rankings of priorities in your life? I, for one, believe that time is our most valuable resource. What do you believe about time?

Let's explore how you invest your time. Give yourself the gift of courage and be radically honest. Your honest assessment will support you. It will lead you to hone your time investment strategies so they are in even more alignment with where you want to go in life.

+ How much time did you spend **today** investing in your dreams and moving in the direction of your dreams, desires, and goals and whatever it is in life that you would like to create and experience more of?

+ How much time did you spend in the **past week** investing in your dreams and moving in the direction of your dreams, desires, and goals and whatever it is in life that you would like to create and experience more of?

+ How much time did you spend in the **past month** investing in your dreams and moving in the direction of your dreams, desires, and goals and whatever it is in life that you would like to create and experience more of?

+ How much time did you spend **today** feeding your distraction, avoidance, busyness, stuckness, or stagnation?

+ How much time did you spend in the **past week** feeding your distraction, avoidance, busyness, stuckness, or stagnation?

+ How much time did you spend in the **past month** feeding your distraction, avoidance, busyness, stuckness, or stagnation?

✦ If you respected time even more how might you invest it differently **today**?

✦ If you respected time even more how might you invest it differently this **week**?

✦ If you respected time even more how might you invest it differently this **month**?

Optimizing Time via the Conduit of Focus

POWER QUOTE

*Productivity comes down to the ability
for you to put your stuff first.*
Mel Robbins

In a world of distractions designed to pull you in a million different directions at once, be a rebel. Master the art of focus by leveraging these time-optimizing techniques:

✦ **Purposefully turn the sound off on your phone and computer when you are working on a project and need to focus.** Turn off anything and everything that may have a visual pop-up notification or a ding sound. The truth is, we are distraction addicts. Know your kryptonite, and do not even allow yourself to drive by the crack house. You dig? Know your own distractions and consciously set yourself up for success ahead of time by creating an environment that lends itself to optimal focus.

✦ **Say no to anything and everything that is not in alignment with where you want to go and who you want to be.** Say yes to what is in alignment. Some people are so busy saying yes to things that don't really matter that they don't even have time to say yes to the things that are the most profound opportunities for growth and forward movement. Strive to have conscious conversations with yourself *before* you say yes or no to anything.

✦ **Take time to pause and reflect on how you are feeling with the invitations you are given.** Ask yourself, *If I say yes to this, what is the actual reason I would be saying yes?* If the reason is FOMO (Fear Of Missing Out), or that you want people to like you, or that you do not want to hurt someone's feelings, or that you would be uncomfortable AF (as f*ck) saying no, then you *know* that you need to say no.

Do the same thing when you are going to say no to something. Get curious and ask yourself why you are saying no. If it is because you know it is going to stretch the shit out of you, or because you will have to face an epic learning curve, or because you are avoiding or putting off your greatness, or because you think you do not have time to do the epic thing because you are too "busy"—even though the things you are busy with aren't what Really Matters (RMs), then say yes and figure it out as you go.

Leverage time by giving yourself permission to pause. Get curious before saying yes or no. This allows you to consciously navigate the directions that you choose as you move through life.

✦ **In an effort to allow yourself the gift of being laser-focused, pick one thing at a time to work on.** Scan the entire room for any potential distractions and make sure to put everything else away. This way you cannot even see anything that might invite your energy to be diverted elsewhere. What might need to be put away in your environment to signal to your mind that you are laser-focused on what you have selected as your one area of focus for now?

✦ **Put systems in place for you to stay accountable.** When working on goals, make sure you have someone else alongside you setting and maintaining a focus on their own goals. This makes the journey more fun. It holds you accountable to what you say you are going to do. It also gives you an outlet to explore when you are falling short of your goals and to discover what resistance is underneath it.

✦ **Set an alarm for a specified amount of time to commit yourself to whatever you're working on.** This way, when your Ninja Mind wants to chatter you know what time to tell it to come back. Say, "Oh, hey Ninja Mind! Hit me up in 20 minutes."

✦ **Schedule time for distractions**. Yep. Schedule time for your own personal favorite distractions.

✦ **Schedule time for errands**. Tackle them at the same time.

✦ **Schedule time for reading emails**.

Do you see a theme here? Be intentional about how you use your time. How might you schedule your time so you can be even more conscious and purposeful as you move through your day?

TAKE YOUR POWER BACK!

What systems might you put in place?
Who might you invite to share the journey?
Who has goals that are in alignment with yours?
How can you create more accountability
for moving toward what you want?

#powerfulAF

The point is this: you get to be the owner of your own time when you stop being so busy reacting to the world around you. If your own Ninja Mind is saying, "Must be nice," then you better check yo-self before you wreck yo-self.

If you believe you are not a Master Creator of time, then you are not. If you give yourself permission to turn that doubt into curiosity, then your whole world transforms. It's time to get curious.

Ask yourself:

✦ What if you were a **Master Creator** of your time?

✦ What might that **look like**?

✦ What might you **do differently**?

✦ How might the version of you that is a Master Creator of time **shift things** to be even more optimal?

✦ How could you **get more out of your day** and enjoy the journey even more?

Beware the Ninja Mind Chatter

When my Ninja Mind chatter starts trying to derail me from my focus and rob me of time, I message a friend and playfully tell on myself. If the chatter keeps going, I have a little talk with the Ninja Mind that goes a little something like this:

Ninja Mind Chatter: "Oh my God, Morgan, we are not going to make the deadline. Holy shit. What are you going to do? This is bad. We are so tired. And hungry. We are so hungry. We don't have time to do it all. You committed to too many things. Why do you always want to stretch and grow so much? Can't you just take a break? Maybe something is wrong with you. I mean, this whole epic and legendary thing is a little too much. You are too much. I feel like good is great, right?

Helloooo? Morgan? Is this thing on? Can you hear me? Wouldn't it be so nice to relax? Can't you just push the project deadline back a few weeks? Then we could take a nap and watch something on Amazon Prime. You deserve a break, Morgan. Oh man, you could take a whole month off. Wouldn't that be so amazing? Or maybe even a whole year off? OMG, dream big Morgan! We could do nothing for a whole year! Anything is possible!"

Conscious Me: "Oh my God, you are so not helpful. The answer is no. And you going on like that is an epic waste of time. You should know by now that I don't listen to your BS. We have six days until deadline, so you can get a break then. Capice? Now, for the love of unicorns and sparkles, can you please be quiet so that I can work my super humanness like I do? Thanks!"

Ninja Mind Chatter: "I feel you, I'll give you a little break, and I'll check in with you later in case you might need my help. Byeeee."

Slow Down to Speed Up: Counter-instinctual, Totally Intuitive

In order to make more time, I slow down. That's right. I slow down to speed up. It sounds, and initially feels, incredibly counter-instinctual. Yet, it is actually quite intuitive. Whenever I am "busy" or overwhelmed and I feel like my world is moving too fast, I start to worry about how I am going to keep up with it all. That is my clue to slow down.

There is a pandemic in our society. We have given way too much power over to our Ninja Minds. We continuously fall into the trap of letting our survival instincts override our inner wisdom, which is always inviting us to live a fully awakened and ignited life. We choose logic over passion and desire. We choose facts over feelings. We choose the Ninja Mind chatter and its enticing lies over the intuitive whispers of the soul.

It is time to choose intuition over instinct. It is time to teach the head to serve the heart. For example, earlier today I was deep in the throes of writing, with deadlines quickly approaching, and also prepping for an event in Indiana where I was a keynote speaker on the topic of power. With the date of my TEDx Talk quickly approaching, I was also juggling the day-to-day responsibilities of my business—one-on-one clients, open enrollments for events and immersion weekends, and the private launch for my Epic Sexy You tank top collection.

My instinct told me to order food to be delivered, which would "save time." At the same time, my intuition gently chimed in and started showing me visions of taking a break to go grocery shopping, cook a yummy, healthy, fresh and nourishing meal for myself, work out, and then get back to writing.

Here's how the conversation between instinct and intuition unfolded:

Instinct: *(energetically frantic and alarmed)* "Are you crazy? You want us to take hours away from working when we already have no time as it is? Have you lost your damn mind?! What we *should* be doing is having more caffeine. Yes. That's the way to go. Crank it up a notch."

Intuition: *(energetically calm, peaceful, and so loving)* "Caffeine overstimulates you, remember? When you are overstimulated you spend hours going down rabbit holes, chasing shiny, endless distractions. The truth is that when we slow down, we speed up. You will have nourishing food, you will hydrate your body with water, take a break, and move your body. Then, when you are done honoring you, you will be amazed at how much more energy you have to give to everything that needs to be done. Slowing down actually gives you more time back. It is hard to explain. It's something you need to experience. So, please, take a chance and trust me? I promise you, you won't regret it." Intuition reaches a hand out to instinct with an invitation to walk down this other path where the euphoric sunshine life awaits.

Instinct: "This is crazy. That is some bullshit. Caffeine sounds like the way to go. It's easier and faster." Twenty minutes later, after some caffeine and staring at the computer screen, having done no work at all, instinct gets curious. "All right, I will try your way just this once. But you better be right."

Two hours later, after a ride in the convertible, some fresh air for the first time in a couple of days, fresh groceries in the fridge, a workout, and the most amazing, made-from-scratch, vegan, gluten-free, soy-free pizza: boom! Magic!! Sure as shit, intuition was on point. It was as if I had gained another 10 hours of energy for the day. This allowed me to work in flow, with absolute focus and ease, well into the wee hours of the night.

Intuition for the win y'all! Intuition for the win!

Counter-instinctual and yet totally intuitive. Give yourself permission to allow your intuition even more space to lead you to the best decisions about how you invest your time. I promise you, you will have your mind blown as you discover what an epic power source your intuition truly is.

Do What Really Matters

POWER QUOTE

It is not enough to be busy.
The question is: What are we busy about?
Henry David Thoreau

With pretty much everything I do I will stop and ask myself, "Is this an intentional investment of my time? Or this a distraction? Is this avoidance? Or is this just busyness masked as something that Really Matters (RMs)?" It's all about getting conscious about why I am doing what I am doing.

Don't get me wrong, there are some days where I say, "I am not going to make any forward moving deposits today. It is my choice. I am taking time to indulge in something that is purely entertainment and allows my mind to shut off for a little while." The point of consciousness is not perfection. Rather, consciousness allows us to stop lying to ourselves.

When we are radically honest and fully conscious, we get to become even more powerful in the ways we navigate the investment of our time. When I catch myself going down a rabbit hole of distraction or I am about to do something that I am well aware is literally wasting life, I ask myself two questions:

✓ *Are you going to regret this?*

✓ *Will you wish you had this time back?*

If the answer to one or both questions is no, then I might give myself a little pocket of time to allow for the distraction. Even so, I try my best to be conscious of my choice. I will often put a time limit on my distraction, so that one hour doesn't become 13 hours of an Amazon Prime binge and then I have wasted an entire day of my life. (Let's just say I have a "friend" who this has happened to. And just so we are clear, by "friend" I mean me.)

I am aware of those times when I am in danger of feeding stuckness and stagnation. However, about 95 percent of the time my answer is, "Yes, yes I will regret this." I then choose to do something that will allow me to feel more proud of me and my time investment strategies.

POWER QUOTE

Time you enjoy wasting was not wasted.
John Lennon

True that, John Lennon. Preach! The only person who can define what it even means to "waste" your time is you. Personally, I enjoy the shit out of laying out in the sun and doing nothing. While others may feel that is a waste of time, I find it to be nourishing and rejuvenating. I am like a crystal that charges in the sun. It feeds my soul.

I also love playing. Some people do not value play as highly as I do; yet, it gives me so much energy. I get so many ideas for soul creations when I am in my fun zone of play. It is a birthplace of magic for me and my business. And it also allows me to cultivate profound connection with myself and others.

TAKE YOUR POWER BACK!

What gives you more energy when you do it?
What is your own definition of time wasted?

#powerfulAF

On the days where I am literally slaying life, I wake up in the morning and check in with myself about what my top direction priorities are. I ask myself, "Which direction am I heading today?" Then I ask, "What is it today that Really Matters (RMs)? What would actually allow me to move in the direction I want to go?"

One of my most powerful habits is to ensure that every single day I take at least one step in the direction I want to go. Take 365 forward steps a year and it will blow your damn mind to see what you are capable of. Infinite possibilities await. What is your one step forward today?

Power Play

You're up! Get out a pen and journal. It's time to get super clear on what RMs (Really Matters).

- ✦ **What activities are you doing where you are literally just wasting your time?** How have you been somehow convincing yourself that these things matter? What are the stories and justifications that your Ninja Mind is telling you as to why those things somehow matter?

✦ **What are your typical distraction mechanisms?** What things keep you from doing the stuff that RMs (Really Matters)?

✦ **Why are you doing what you are doing in each moment of the day?** What is the intention behind or beneath your choice to do each thing?

✦ **Why are you spending time with the people you are spending time with?** Is it because they feed your soul or is it out of familiarity, obligation, and patterning? Give yourself the gifts of curiosity and consciousness. With awareness comes the opportunity to make new choices that lead to new versions of you who have access to even more possibilities.

✦ **What do you truly want in life?** What are the things that Really Matter (RM) in moving you toward that desire?

In a relationship you may be spending time physically co-existing with one another, but is that what you want? Do you want more? If so, what are some things that you could do that would Really Matter (RM) in moving you consciously and proactively towards that more? How might the two of you co-create more consciousness, presence, and connection in your relationship?

Remember to focus on you, your part, what you can do. You cannot change others but you absolutely have the power to change your part.

In coaching many entrepreneurs and life coaches (and in being one myself), I see just how much we lie to ourselves when it comes to the activities that we do in the course of a day. As if focusing on the website or the business cards are going to be what RMs. When what Really Matters is having conversations to invite people to work with you. How many people did you invite to have a conversation with you today?

The Ninja Mind is going to respond with something like, "I invited three people to have a conversation today, so leave me be." My follow-up question would be, "Do those people know that the intention of the conversation is about business?" If not, then you've got some energetic cleaning up to do. That is a whole separate book, so make sure that you go to the Epic Sexy You website right now at www.epicsexyyou.com. Sign up at the bottom of the homepage to be sure you are in the know when that book for entrepreneurs becomes available.

Keep giving yourself permission to be radically honest about how you are investing your time. Every day strive for an even more powerful and profitable allocation of your time.

Power Play

Get out that journal and pick your very favorite pen. Go back through this entire section on time and reflect.

✦ **Which ideas are you most pulled toward?** Which ones would you most like to try on and play with so that you can be even more masterful in your conscious use of time?

✦ **What are some of your own ideas?** What are some possibilities that would allow you to shift your current time investment strategies and make them even more profitable?

If at any point you find yourself buying into the illusion that you are powerless to time or never seem to have enough of it, revisit this section. Consciously play with all the ways that you can become a Master Creator of time.

TAKE YOUR POWER BACK!

Time can either be compounding in the direction of your dreams or in the direction of stagnation. The choice is yours. Choose your dreams. You are so damn worth it.

#powerfulAF

POWER SOURCE #8

THE VORTEX OF TRUTH

POWER QUOTE

Denial is the shock absorber for the soul.
It protects us until we are equipped
to cope with reality.
C.S. Lewis

Most people think that the opposite of truth is lying. I would say that statement is way too obvious. I would say that the opposite of truth is denial. The most dangerous and damaging lies we tell are the ones we tell ourselves. The most dangerous and damaging secrets are the ones we keep from ourselves.

Ooooo yes, denial. But denial allows you to stay ignorantly blissful for only so long. If you truly want a life beyond your wildest dreams, you're going to have to get radically honest with yourself and everyone around you.

There is so much power in truth; it affords you the freedom to be you. When you master the art of truth with self and others, you will feel the heavy load that lifts from you. Secrecy breeds shame. When we hide things, whether from ourselves or others, it weighs us down. Lies, denial, and omissions are like bricks tied to our legs, and we are pulled down while fighting to keep our head above the surface. It is exhausting.

Truth is the epicenter of authenticity, and authenticity is the epicenter of power. True power lies in the freedom to be you, unapologetically. To own all of you. To stop hiding and dare to shine bright. To own your epic feats. To do whatever you want, when you want, and how you want to do it. To own your darkness. To set yourself free.

POWER QUOTE

Truth is like the sun. You can shut it out for a time, but it ain't goin' away.
Elvis Presley

Uniquely, Unapologetically You

Let's talk a little bit more about how, over the course of time, you are conditioned into the art of hiding your true self. You receive subliminal messages when you are a child that make you feel as if somehow you can't express all of yourself. You learn that certain parts of you are "good" and certain parts of you are "bad." It is not intentional on your parents' part. Often it is wrapped in what is thought to be love and protection; yet, what it teaches you is to hide.

The message you get is to hide pieces of who you are. Don't show those pieces to the world. Be calculated on what you show and to whom you show it. Don't stand out too much. Don't be too much. Eventually you learn that you will be "safer" in hiding— safer as in you will care way too much what other people think. Your caregivers' own subconsciously embedded caveman survival instincts sent you this subliminal protection message: hide or else you might get eaten by that lion, tiger, or bear—oh, my!

SPOTLIGHT STORY

When you step into your own Vortex of Truth, you will experience life in a whole new lane of freedom and liberation. Let me share a personal story with you to illustrate this point. Although your own story may be a bit different from mine, I can assure you that you are hiding some parts of you from yourself and/or from the world.

For me, at some point in my growth journey, it became glaringly obvious that in order for me to grow to the next level of awakening and become even more of the person I wanted to be, I needed to stop hiding. But one of my biggest fears at the beginning of my journey to becoming a public thought leader was what others would think of me if I showed up fully and authentically as me.

I was especially afraid of what my parents would think of me. I was afraid that if I stepped out into the world as who I actually was I would somehow disappoint or embarrass them by exposing some of the parts of me that had been in hiding for so long. I knew, based on those subliminal messages I had received as a child, that the world may not accept my choice to be so public about some parts of me and that I may actually be perceived as "bad" or "weird" or "crazy."

The truth was, since I was a young child, I have walked in two realms. I have always had one foot (or at the very least a toe) in the human realm and one foot (or often the majority of myself) in the spiritual realm. I have seen spirits. I hear them. I get visions. I am an awakened portal—a conduit who communicates directly with the guidance of beings not of this world.

As a kid, I tried telling my parents about this many times. I remember trying to talk to my parents about "the people in the basement," spirits who were not a fan of being bothered by kids playing down there. When I would bring it up, I could tell they thought I was just making up pretend stories.

I remember being told as a child that I had a "wild imagination" and that I was "dramatic." I was a big personality and still am. But when those words were used with regard to me expressing my realities of living in two realms, I felt dismissed, unheard, and unseen. I felt wrong and bad—not just that what I was saying was bad, but that who I was was somehow bad.

Again, I am well aware that this was in no way, shape, form, or fashion their intent; yet, this was the way my not yet fully developed child brain processed the feedback I was receiving from them about who I should and should not be. As an adult, I decided to reparent those small and confused but majestic pieces of me. I began having conversations with friends, family, clients, and even my parents about who I really was. I came out of hiding. I invited my parents to have a conversation with me where they got to hear me reveal to them fully—unapologetically and unfiltered—who I actually was.

I let them know that I was no longer interested in hiding my magic or any parts of me from the world. It was a proclamation to myself that it was time to own who I was fully and not give so much a shit about what others thought about me, including them. God love them, their patience, and their ongoing adaptation to having such a soulfully rebellious, trailblazing daughter!

Coming out of the spiritual closet to my parents, my family, my friends, and my clients was one of the absolute hardest and also most liberating things I have ever done. I was so afraid that people would think I was crazy, which of course some did and some still do. Yet, the magic that it opened up in my life was profound. People started opening up to me about things that were hiding in their own closets.

One of the coolest things that happened, one I didn't even see coming, is that I became a magnet for others who were awakening to or were already awakened to their own spiritual magic.

Here's the thing: when you identify your own areas of hiding and you give yourself the gift of being authentically and unapologetically you, you give others permission to do the same. When you are not hiding who you are, you will find that you become a conduit of truth for others to get to come play in your world without their masks. Do you know what a gift that is to yourself and to every single soul who comes in contact with you?

The power of truth is about being seen for who you actually are. If I had not come out of the spiritual closet to my parents, I would have been robbing them of the opportunity to get to know who I actually am. I had to let go of who others thought I was and stop hiding in order to give myself, my parents, my clients, and anyone else in my stratosphere an opportunity to see the rawest expression of my truth, authenticity, and magic.

If you want to be seen, you have to have the courage to show the world who you truly are. Sometimes truth is about unbecoming who you think you need to be for the world around you so that you can become who you actually are. Truth is about connecting with radical authenticity and expressing with the fullest honesty of self. Truth is about being in complete alignment—mind, words, thoughts, actions, energy, body, and soul. When it all matches up, you will have an endless source of energy and time back in your life, meaning you can get busy living.

You will be amazed when you realize how much work it was to hide who you are. I know it is scary and, yes, you may be judged. You may lose some people who are close to you. But if they don't love you and accept you for who you really are, did you ever truly have a genuine connection with them in the first place? Give yourself and the world the gift of the most epic power source of all, which is the truth of you.

Power Play

Get out that journal and get to writing! It's time for some epic, self-exploratory truth bombs to take your power back and set you free. Let's explore where and how you might be hiding in life so that you can step into your very own Truth Vortex.

+ What are some of the **closets you hide in**?

+ What parts of you do you **hide from others**?

+ What parts of you do you **hide from yourself**?

+ What might it look like to share more of **your fullest expression** of yourself with the world? Unedited. Unfiltered. No hiding.

+ Who might you share **more of your authentic self** with?

+ If you were to get incredibly honest with yourself, what are some of the **lies you might be telling** yourself?

+ What are some of the **lies you are telling others**?

✦ If you were to start living life **anchored in even more truth**, what might that look like? How might you show up differently?

✦ Watch where you get the most defensive. Know that **defensiveness** is often a portal for epic soul growth.

✦ Let's talk **"Little White Lies,"** defined by the *Merriam-Webster Dictionary* as "a lie about a small or unimportant matter that someone tells to avoid hurting another person." What are the "Little White Lies" that you tell others?

✦ What are some of the **reasons, justifications, and rationalizations** for each little white lie you tell?

✦ What are the **little white lies** that you tell yourself?

✦ In what areas of your life do you feel you are **lying to yourself**? What might it look like to add more honesty into those areas?

✦ In what areas of your life do you feel you are **lying to others**? What might it look like to add more honesty into those areas?

✦ Where in your life are you **lying via omission**? Where are you not sharing all of the details of truth with others and then lying to yourself or convincing yourself that somehow you are actually being honest when, in fact, you are not? What is this pattern costing you? Get curious as to what you are avoiding in not giving the full truth. And what might be different in life if you decided to commit to full transparency and radical honesty moving forward?

Give yourself permission to face your own truths. Own who you are fully and unapologetically. Feel how you really feel. Want what you really want. Know what you really know. If you want more, own it. If you're unhappy, own it. If you're not a hell yes in your relationship or your job or business, own it.

At the very least, stop lying to yourself about it. Be honest with yourself. Yes, it's scary and vulnerable and confusing. And then it's liberating AF (As F*ck).

TAKE YOUR POWER BACK!

Every lie you tell buries your true self,
whereas honesty sets you free to be
Who you really are and makes space
for the Who you are becoming.

#powerfulAF

III

RECAP

LET'S RECAP, SHALL WE?!

POWER QUOTE

Self-mastery is the first step towards
attaining enlightenment.
Kilroy J. Oldster, Dead Toad Scrolls

First of all, epic celebration that you made it here! Stop and celebrate the courage that it took for you to work through all of the questions posed in this book, exploring each and every Take Your Power Back and working through the deep soul excavation exercises available to you in each and every Power Play. You are clearly committed to self-mastery and to becoming an even more powerful Master Creator of your life.

This book has been an ongoing invitation to step into more and more of your limitless power. There is an infinite supply of power available to you here. Come back to this book again and again. This is your vortex of truth. It is your path to ever-evolving expansion. Every single time that you read any piece of this book, you will gain access to new versions of you where even more epic possibilities await.

It is time that we stop giving the best of us to whatever pays the bills, the rest of us to our loved ones, and then—*if* there is anything left to give—to ourselves. We've got it all backwards. Focusing on self-mastery is compounding. No one can take anything from you unless you let them. Your house could burn down and be gone in a day. You could lose your job. Something unexpected could happen and wipe out your bank account. A relationship might end. But once you've discovered your true power within, nothing will ever be able to take it from you unless you allow it.

This journey is about awakening to and fully owning your true power—the unmistakable, unlimited power that is right there inside you right now. Now that you get that power is an inside job and you have the tools to tap into it, you will realize there are no mistakes. It is all happening *for you* and in service to your expansion and growth.

You now have a choice.

You can keep perpetuating the subconscious mediocrity given to you from the outside world or you can decide to live fully with whatever time you have left. It is never too late to get busy living. I cannot wait to see what you do with this wisdom. Playing small stops now. It is time to be all that you are, to own it and get busy living the life you've always dreamed of living, one tiny step forward at a time.

Remember that every single question that was posed in every yummy nook and cranny of this book is a portal to new possibilities. If you explore answering even just one question a day from this book, every day for the next year, your entire life will radically transform. You literally will not even recognize your life one year from now.

What question are you going to choose to explore today?

The most powerful way to create and sustain this ever expanding inner power is to share the journey. Who do you know that needs to read this book? Who in your life would benefit from this vortex of truth and sharing the journey of expansion with you? Who will you invite to join you? Who might benefit from the wisdom you now have?

Imagine a whole world full of people around you who own their power and do not try to steal yours, because they now know better. Give yourself and others the gift of unshakable power and worth. Invite others into this new truth with you so that together you can truly thrive.

And finally, remember...

P *Power is an inside job.* Think for yourself.

O *Own what is yours.* Hand back what is not.

W *Walk the talk.* Alignment and authenticity are game changers.

E *Everything in your life* is in your wheelhouse of creation. You are the Master Creator.

R *Revel in the magic* of new possibilities for power.

Bet on you. You are so worth it!

XOXO
Morgan

241

HOW TO SQUEEZE THE JUICINESS OUT OF THIS SOUL BOOK

POWER QUOTE

Repetition is the mother of mastery.
Unknown

This is not a one and done kind of book. This book was created with the intention that it would be a guidebook for you to return to over and over again on your journey to more power, more happiness, more fulfillment, more abundance, more love for self and life and others, and more joy.

Evolution is a process. You will never be "there." "There" is a myth. Even if "there" existed, I can assure you that you would be bored out of your ever-living mind. The growth and expansion that is available to you in this lifetime is infinite, and it requires ongoing commitment and exploration.

Every single time you read this book you will be reading it as a new version of you. Each time, you will find more depths of power available to you. So come back to this book again and again.

Do the Work!

No matter what you choose to do, remember that you do not learn how to swim while sitting beside the pool reading about swimming. You learn how to swim by getting in the swimming pool. Stretch yourself. Get in the metaphorical pool of life. You will learn with every bit of water you swallow. Every single time water goes up your nose, you own a little bit more of your power.

What appears to be a struggle is often a lesson. As you encounter your very own water-up-your-nose moments, ask yourself, "What is this trying to teach me?" Then, course correct from there. I have personally learned over and over and over again (and over and over and over again) that it takes more energy to avoid the work than it does to do the work.

You learn by doing. Do the work.

Progress, Not Perfection

Focus on progress, not perfection. Remember that the evolution of you and your expanding into more and more Power is a lifelong adventure, not a destination or end point. Do not let waiting for perfection get in the way of you doing the work.

You do not need to know every single step on the path ahead in order to take the first step. Take the first step, and you will find that that step will inform the next step.

This is not about having all of the puzzle pieces of power in your hands and knowing how they all fit together before you ever experience true power. Rather, allow yourself the opportunity and privilege of learning about each piece one at a time. Give yourself the gift of presence and take the time to play with and integrate each piece one at a time. Enjoy your unique experience of growth, celebrate each day's progress of moving forward, and reclaim your power day by day.

When you are feeling stuck or lost, make it a habit to look back at how far you've come. You may find that you frequently experience what I affectionately refer to as Awesomeness Amnesia. The anecdote of forgetting how badass you are is to look back at where you started and celebrate how far you've come. Look back at every step you took and all the moments of growth you've experienced along the way.

You are more of a badass than your Ninja Mind will ever have you believe. Once you remember how badass you are and just how far you have already come, you can get back to choosing courage over fear. Reconnected to your Power Source, you will find yourself back in the forward flow of movement.

Remember, perfection is not a realistic, achievable, or attainable thing, so place your focus on progress and forward momentum, take baby steps and celebrate your growth. That is what this journey is all about.

One Thing at a Time

Pick one thing at a time. Play with that as your central focus for learning and mastery, application and implementation. Every day, dedicate yourself to stretching and growing into that one thing. Rome was not built in a day. It was built one foundational piece at a time. It is time to be the master architect of your life. It's time to lay an unshakable foundation of power to build your epic and legendary life upon.

If at any time you try something on and it just doesn't feel like it's your jam, give yourself permission to discard it and move on. Remember, this is about you finding what works for you. Do not blindly follow a path to power that anyone or anything, even this book, leads you to if it does not feel right for you.

Create your own path to power by doing what feels good and exploring what works for you. Determine what "works" by considering those things that allow you to grow and expand, to evolve and step more and more into your boldest and brightest expression of power. There is no one-size-fits-all anything in life. Give yourself the gift of being uniquely you and honoring your way unapologetically.

Keep the Growth Partaaay Going and Come Play with Me!

We all deserve to experience a life fully awakened. Gift yourself and others the spark of awakening. I'd love to invite you to watch and share the TEDx Talk that I did with TEDxOakParkWomen that was the foundation for this book. You can find it at www.epicsexyyou.com.

For even more depths of power and mind-blowing expansion, I invite you to come play with me! Go to the website and enter your email at the bottom of the page to be in the know on all new things as they launch. Check out the events, retreats, weekend immersions, and online group programs on the website. There are programs for entrepreneurs, intuitives, life coaches, and lightworkers. Choose from programs such as: Intuitive Life Coaches Training, Magic Sparkle Boundaries, Epic Book Writing, The Epic Art of Avatars, Awakening the Intuitive Within, and Dream Incubator for Soulpreneurs. Additional programs currently in development include offerings for those seeking love and abundance in epic proportions.

Drop your email on the Epic Sexy You website to make sure you are in the know for details on how to tune in to the *Powerful As F*ck* Podcast that is currently in the soul cooker. If you have questions and or ideas for topics that you would like covered in more depth, email me and we will add them to the queue of creation and inspiration.

Be sure to check out my first Book *Epic Sexy You: No Limits. No Rules.* You will find it on Amazon, for print and Kindle, and on Audible for the audiobook version.

If you would like to work together one-on-one for private coaching or to inquire about having me as a speaker at an event, contributing to your publication, or interviewing me for TV, radio, podcast, articles, or blogs, reach me at morgan@epicsexyyou.com.

✦ *Get Connected, Join the Tribe.* ✦

Follow on Instagram: **@epicsexyyou**

Like on Facebook: **facebook.com/epicsexyyou**

Like on Facebook: **facebook.com/officialmorganfield**

Subscribe on YouTube: **EpicSexyYou**

Author Bio

Morgan Field is the author of the six-time award-winning, Amazon best-selling book, *Epic Sexy You: No Limits. No Rules.* She is an award-winning and internationally recognized Intuitive Life Coach, TEDx Speaker, Writer, and Keynote Speaker who plays in the artistry of alchemy, turning subconscious blocks into catalysts of forward movement and alchemizing your darkness, your fears, and your comfort zone into the playground of light that guides your path of metamorphosis and stretches you into a whole new world of infinite possibilities.

She is the Founder of the global empowerment movement, Epic Sexy You, which is currently in 20 countries and counting. She helps you learn how to access infinite possibilities so that you can have it ALL—unshakable confidence, power from the inside out, business success, epic love, wealth, health, authentically radical self love, bountiful bliss and joy, and anything and everything else you crave to experience, be, and have—***no sacrifices, no settling***.

Epic Sexy You's mission is to help you create an Epic and Legendary Life you absolutely love living. Through one-on-one coaching, soulfully explosive immersion weekends, virtual group programs, online DIY courses, and live events, the movement is focused on teaching you how to access a version of yourself you fiercely love being; to get to feel sexy, radiant, and confident from the inside out; to chase fiercely wild and epic dreams; and to shed all that society has conditioned you into so that you can truly become authentically, unapologetically *You* as you leave your epic light legacy imprint on the world.

Powerful Gratitude

Erin—I am so grateful to have experienced 15 years of a wild ride of friendship with you, with an epic lifetime of adventures still ahead. Every single day I am overwhelmed with gratitude and love for you and our journey together. I am eternally grateful for the ebbs and flows that always lead us back to one another and make us even stronger every single time. I am grateful that you let me be my expansive self and share the soul messages that come through for you, even when you tell me to GFY. I love your sense of humor and honor, admire, and appreciate your determination to get back up every single time you fall. God bless the superhumanness that you are as a mother. The courage it takes to continuously strive for conscious parenting is profound, and your powerful happy nuggets are such a gift to the world. I love you so much. Thank you for being a part of my life. My world is a better place for having you in it.

Shawna—Holy shitballs, am I ever so grateful for the magic that is our divinely expansive and cosmically explosive partnership. My mind is blown every single day by what we have co-created over the years. You helped me find my way back to me. You are an endless source of truth and tough love that allows me to continually expand into versions of me that I didn't even think I was capable of or had not yet dared to imagine. I feel so damn blessed to have you in my life. Thank you for being the epic fireworker that you are and for helping me learn to dance in the fire of life, where a whole new realm of possibility awaits me. This book, the TEDx Talk, and living in majestic Miami were all leaps that you were an invaluable asset in helping me create. I love you so much. Thank you!!!

Heidi—Thank you for being a source of energetic balance for this soul creation. You are the gentle to my direct, the infinite compassion to my epic truth bombs, and the cocoon in which I got to sort through it all to allow this book to become whatever it wanted to be.

Dawn—Thank you for saying yes to round two of powerful, soulful co-creation. All the signs and divine wisdom greenlighted us to share this magical journey together yet again. I am so grateful to you and the care that you take in helping birth soul creations.

Julie Scott, Jane Kim England, Lana Williams, and Tiffany Nicole—Thank you for being the pioneers of the Epic Book Writing Program. I am honored and blessed to have gotten to share the journey and accountability of birthing my soul creation alongside yours. What a wild ride, ladies! This is just the beginning for us all! WOO! Infinite possibilities ahead! Cosmically and infinitely grateful for each of you! Xoxo

Alan Griffin, Cora Boyd, John Drumgoole Jr, Joe Giangrasso, Theora Moench, Christopher Kenneth Thomas, Liz Corwin, Melissa Coglianese, Bill Carmody, Sivan Katz, Jennifer Knappe, Elaine Grace, Lee Gaitan, Amber Strong, Diana Hernandez, Nick J Murphy, Kalena James, Kat V, Dr. Cristian Pavel, Michelle Royal, Ilena Adamson, JoAnn S. Brown, Nancy Rae Allen—To everyone who did a reader testimonial, pre-reads, provided ideas and feedback, and helped me soul jam on the essence of this book, thank you infinitely!!! Co-creating with a powerful tribe is so much more magical than going at it alone. Thank you, thank you, thank you!!!

Pops—You pioneered a path of unapologetic authenticity and endless pursuits of striving for more and more self-mastery throughout this adventure of life. You are a true alchemist of transmuting darkness into light and teaching people how to advocate for themselves and own their power. The legacy imprint that you have left and continue to leave on the world is mind-blowing. I am honored to call you my father. I love you.

Mom—You have an epic sense of humor and you pioneered a path of possibility through writing with your creative, playful, and funny holiday newsletters. You are also the person that I handed my power away to the most in life before I awakened to my own true knowingness of what power is. Thank you for your patience in my years of having Power Tangled up with you. I love you, thank you, please forgive me, I'm sorry. It is my greatest wish for you to continually expand into more and more and more of your own epic power and to give yourself permission to be the fullest and most unapologetic expression of the majestic being that you are. Your persistence in your own growth journey is inspiring and admirable. You are courageous AF (as f*ck) and I honor you. Keep growing, sister friend. Nothing is impossible. Dream big!

Sean—I genuinely desire for you to get to experience on an even deeper level the infinite and profound power that you are. My greatest wish for you is for you to become even more of a Master Creator of your life and get to unleash even more love and joy for yourself. I hope you get to experience everything and anything you desire in life. You are so worth it. You are so powerful. Your kids are two of my favorite souls of all time. Being Aunti MoMo is one of my favorite Whos I have ever had the pleasure of being in my life. I love you. Thank you.

Gratitude to My Tribe—Every single day I wake up filled with overwhelming gratitude and joy that I get to work with the clients that I do. I pinch myself daily that I have an epic tribe of souls that allows me the honor to be the sacred cocoon of expansion for your deepest and most powerful growth. I am so incredibly inspired by you and blessed beyond belief that I have the absolute pleasure of working with and sharing this dream chasing adventure of life with you. Thank you infinitely from the bottom of my heart and soul. I am such a lucky and blessed woman, and I wake up filled with so much bliss and joy as a result of knowing that I get to share the journey with you! Love love love love love me some you!!

Jen, Lennon, and Riley—Love you so much!!! My heart and soul is filled with gratitude daily to get to have you all in my life! I want nothing more than for you each to get to step into your fullest power and to experience the profound depths of love and abundance that await you as you manifest your dreams! Thank you for being you! xoxo

.

CPSIA information can be obtained
at www.ICGtesting.com
Printed in the USA
FFHW011711100719
53538341-59194FF